COMPUTER GRAPHICS

BY THE SAME AUTHOR

COMPUTER GRAPHICS
How It Works, What It Does

LARRY KETTELKAMP

Morrow Junior Books / New York

PHOTO CREDITS

Permission for photographs is gratefully acknowledged: Aldus Corporation, p. 51; Anakin Research, Inc., p. 27; Apple Computer, Inc., pp. 33, 60, 81; AutoDesk, Inc., p. 70; CalComp, p. 28; Carlbom and Paciorek, p. 69; Cemax, Inc., pp. 87, 88; CGL, Inc., pp. 3, 97, 103; Codonics, p. 58; Cubicomp Corporation, p. 72; DataDesk International, p. 21; Electronic Arts, pp. 50, 106; Environmental Systems Research Institute, p. 62 (bottom); Herbert Freeman/John Ahn, pp. 61, 65; Geobased Systems, Inc., p. 10; Houston Instrument Division, AMETEK, Inc., pp. 39, 40; Inscribe, Inc., p. 36; Kensington Microware, p. 25; Macworld, January 1988, pp. 35, 45; Marburg/Art Resource, N.Y., p. 84; Mimetics, Inc./Electronic Arts, p. 78; Mindscape Inc., pp. 112, 114, 115; Pitman Learning, Inc., p. 62 (top); George Rorick/Knight-Ridder Graphics, p. 54; Scala/Art Resource, N.Y., p. 84; Mona/ Leo by Lillian Schwartz, Software Gerard Holzman, Lilyan Productions, p. 85; Scitex Corporation, Ltd., p. 75; Silicon Beach Software, pp. 55, 99, 109; Sony Corporation of America, p. 16; The Company, Inc., p. 38; Versatec, Inc., p. 42; Ziff-Davis Publishing Company, pp. 23, 26, 30.

Printed in the United States of America.
1 2 3 4 5 6 7 8 9 10

Library of Congress Cataloging-in-Publication Data

Kettelkamp, Larry.
Computer graphics : how it works, what it does / by Larry
Kettelkamp.
p. cm.
Includes index.
Summary: Explores the science and technology of computer graphics,
how computer videogames and animations work, and how computer
graphics are used in communications, design, science, and medicine.
ISBN 0-688-07504-5
1. Computer graphics—Juvenile literature. [1. Computer
graphics.] I. Title.
T385.K48 1989
006.6—dc 19 88-38924 CIP AC

ACKNOWLEDGMENTS

The author wishes to thank the following persons for contributing materials and offering helpful suggestions:

Herbert Freeman, New Jersey Professor of Computer Engineering and Director of the Center for Computer Aids for Industrial Productivity, Rutgers University, New Brunswick, N.J.

John Ahn, Consultant, AT&T Bell Laboratories, Holmdel, N.J.

Michael Klouda, Computer Consultant, Newtown, Pa.

Frank Rivera, Professor, Coordinator of Computer Graphics Program, Mercer County Community College, Trenton, N.J.

David Crawford, Assistant Professor, Technology Division, Mercer County Community College, Trenton, N.J.

Mary Barber, Senior Technical Assistant, Mercer County Community College, Trenton, N.J.

Edward Stein, Professor, Learning Center Chairperson for Performing and Visual Arts, Brookdale Community College, Lincroft, N.J.

Lori Uffer, Instructor, Art Department, Brookdale Community College, Lincroft, N.J.

Susan Sparks, Production Director, Computer Graphics Laboratory, New York Institute of Technology, Old Westbury, N.Y.

Karlyn Ford, Media Specialist, Lafayette, Calif.

Thomas Simonet, Professor of Journalism, Rider College, Lawrenceville, N.J.

George Rorick, Graphics Department, Knight-Ridder Syndicate, Washington, D.C.

Lillian Feldman Schwartz, Consultant, Computer Graphics, Film, and Video, AT&T Bell Laboratories

To my sister, Karlyn,
whose images reach beyond the screen

CONTENTS

INTRODUCTION

Computer graphics is a new science. It is a way of using the computer and its display screen to create pictures ranging from line drawings to animations, from black-and-white photographs to the most complicated color images used in modern printing. Fine artists use the computer to create their art. Engineers use computer-aided design to plan new machines. Architects model buildings with computer images. Mathematicians illustrate complex forms. Cartographers use data stored in computers to make charts and maps. Doctors scan the inside of the body and view it in three dimensions with the use of computer graphics. Scientists depend on computer graphics to analyze and clarify photographs of the earth and planets. Newspaper and magazine editors and artists design page layouts by computer. Musicians write their music on the computer screen. Instructors use computer graphics as teaching aids in the classroom and as simulators to train automobile drivers and airline pilots. Young and old alike use computer graphics for the pure enjoyment of making original drawings and designs of every sort. And almost everyone enjoys video games. In short, there is little in modern life that is not affected in some way by the remarkable technology of computer graphics.

In the following chapters you can read how computer video games and animations work, and how computer graphics is used in communications, design, science, and medicine.

1

A NEW SCIENCE

☐ COMPUTER GRAPHICS IS BORN ☐

Developments in computer graphics parallel developments in computers in general. However, certain highlights have contributed to the explosion of interest in this new science.

In the early 1950s computers were huge machines that used vacuum tubes. Banks of equipment filled entire rooms. During this era pioneering work in computer graphics was done at the Massachusetts Institute of Technology. There the huge Whirlwind computer was used to create moving images of aircraft that were part of the government's strategic air defense system called SAGE. In 1955 a faster and more compact TX series computer was developed for research, and in 1956 came a special development that was to lead to computer graphics as we know it today. That year an engineer named Ivan Sutherland invented the "sketch pad." The principle involved a stylus moved over a tablet or a light-sensitive pen held against the computer screen. In either case a grid translated independent movements of the tool into lines drawn on the computer screen. A line could be extended and the end of it shifted to any angle. Lines could be connected to represent solid objects. And, amazingly, the drawn objects then could be slowly rotated in three dimensions so that certain lines disappeared or came into view in a natural way. In 1961 an inventor named Steve Russell created a computer game called Space War. In his game rocket orbits interacted with the same timing that would take place if the rockets had actually been fired. However, the game had to be played on a large system that cost $120,000 for the computer alone, so it was never marketed.

In the early 1970s the University of Utah became an experimental center for computer graphics. There Ivan Sutherland worked with a number of gifted graduate students. Computerized "wireframe" images were developed to outline and divide the planes of complex organic surfaces such as a human hand or face. A student named Fred Fox computerized an animated and talking head. Sutherland created a complex animation of a rocking horse. The image on the screen was multiplied and manipulated so that independent horses appeared to rock in their own rhythms and horses in the foreground were brighter than those in the background. Sutherland and his students went on to refine their animations to include objects with "smooth curves." And

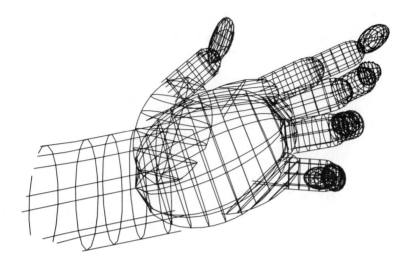

A wireframe hand for 3-D animation.

ten points were arranged in a grid pattern on the surface of the object to create lighting and highlight effects.

One of the students at the University of Utah was Nolan Bushnell. He was familiar with games of the amusement-park industry, including arcade games, and he invented similar games to play on the university's $8 million computer. Bushnell foresaw that when equipment became more practical and less expensive, the computer and the arcade-game industry would become natural partners. As a result Nolan Bushnell developed the first practical video arcade game in the late 1970s. He called his new game Pong®, and it is still popular today.

Although the most important early developments were

3

made in engineering labs, and remained there, by the late 1970s computers had become small enough and cheap enough that computer graphics suddenly caught on as a popular field of computer technology. Books, technical journals, and popular magazines appeared, all introducing and educating the public to the new possibilities. Schools offered computer graphics courses. Video arcades sprang up in shopping malls, and video entertainment and education packages were developed for home use. Would-be artists of all ages took to the computer. Computer graphics had arrived.

☐   **SCREENS AND PIXELS**   ☐

A computer works by recognizing on and off electrical impulses represented by changes in voltage. The "on" position is represented by the digit 1, and the "off" position is represented by the digit 0. Since only two digits are used, the system is called *binary,* from the term "bi," which means two. In computer terms each number is called a *bit,* short for "binary digit." A series consisting usually of eight bits is called a *byte.* Series consisting of 8, 16, 24, 32, 36, 48, 60, or 64 bits are called *words.* This simple system can represent all common numbers as well as complex collections of information. It is the foundation language in which computers speak and from which they construct their images.

In order to perform its tasks the computer must have *memory.* Microcircuits must contain enough "switches" so that large groups of bytes and words can be temporarily stored as information or commands. Most tasks require at least several thousand bytes. The number 1,000 can be written as "kilo," so such a computer is often said to have a certain number of *kilobytes* of memory. More complex computers require *megabytes*, or millions of bytes. Kilo is shortened to K and mega to M, and a computer is described as having so many K bytes or M bytes in its memory storage bank.

The image on a computer screen is produced by a *cathode-ray tube*, or CRT for short. It is a sealed bottle from which all the air has been removed to allow electrons to travel freely. The bottle is narrow at one end and flares out at the other to form the wide, slightly curved surface you see as a video screen.

In a CRT (cathode-ray tube), the heated cathode generates a beam of negative electrons, which is attracted toward a positive anode. The beam is focused and deflected to the screen, causing the phosphors to glow.

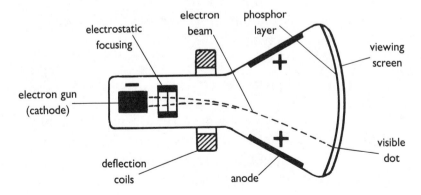

At the narrow end is an electron gun in which a heated unit called a cathode is made to emit electrons. At opposite sides of the wide end of the tube are materials that form an anode. The anode has a positive electrical charge—that is, it needs electrons. Since electrons are units of negative charge, they are attracted toward the anode from the cathode in a high-speed stream. Magnetic coils in the middle of the tube deflect the beam to aim it as it passes by. The deflected beam of electrons strikes light-absorbing chemicals called *phosphors* that coat the inside of the screen at the end of the tube, causing them to glow. The glowing phosphors appear as an image seen from the outside of the screen.

The phosphors are arranged in rows of dots. Each glowing dot is a picture element, called *pixel* for short. Light from groups of dots is blended by the eye to appear as a continuous image. The smoothness of this image depends partly on how far the observer is from the screen. An image viewed up close will look more coarse, or dotted, than one viewed from farther away. Smoothness also depends on the number of pixels that fit into one complete row across the screen and the number of horizontal rows that are stacked to fill the screen.

☐   **COMPUTER GRAPHICS SYSTEMS**   ☐

Several components combine to form a computer graphics system. The first of these is a host computer. This holds what is called an application program and provides the data needed for creating a graphic image. Through a two-way

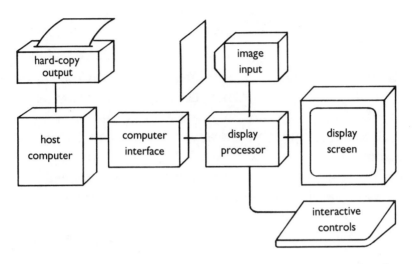

A computer graphics system includes a host computer, a computer interface, a display processor and screen, interactive controls, and a linkage to image input and output.

digital link called an *interface,* the host computer is connected to the graphics terminal. The terminal includes a display processor, a display monitor screen, and the controls that interact with them. It is the job of the display processor to both create and "refresh" the image on the screen. This special image, or display file, is stored in a temporary or *buffer memory.* From there it can be repeatedly sent to the display screen either to maintain or modify the image. The display processor allows the image to be quickly created and held as a stable picture or erased and replaced. To do this it has to handle several aspects or parameters of the image. These include the number of pixels on the screen, the intensity or brightness of the image, whether or not more than one color is used, how easily the image can be erased, and how fast the image can be "written" across the screen. Another parameter is called "linearity." This is the ability to create and display lines that are clear and precise in terms of their length, direction, and angle on the display screen.

A computer must have a way to hold in its memory the digital information that allows it to operate. Although the basic storage unit is the byte, today's computers work in terms of megabytes, or M bytes. Personal computers may have as many as sixteen M bytes of memory, and somewhat more complex minicomputers can have many times that capacity.

Besides internal memory and the buffer memory that keeps an image on the screen, the computer also needs extra memory storage. This may be in the form of reels of magnetic tape for the large installations called mainframe computers. Or it may be in the form of hard or soft *disks* for more compact systems. Most common are the soft or floppy diskettes. They come in 8-inch, 5.25-inch, and 3.5-inch diameters. Floppy disks look like small phonograph records but instead of grooves they have circular bands containing magnetic particles. A disk is fed into a slot in a transport device called a disk drive, often located beside or beneath the display screen. There it rotates while a magnetic head moves to the correct sector where magnetic information is to be added or retrieved. Information can be almost instantly "read" no matter where it was recorded on the disk. Both sides of a floppy disk can hold magnetic information and it can be erased and replaced many times. Specially prepared programs of memory information and commands on floppy disks are called *software,* and many of these are now available for computer graphics.

New laser disks for computer memory are now also coming into use. They are comparable to the CDs used for sound recording. One type is called WORM, meaning "Write Once Read Many." The computer disk can be recorded on once and then played back any number of times. Another type, just on the market, can be erased and recorded on any number of times.

Computer graphics components are connected by means of a linkage called an *interface.* One type, called serial, sends one bit of information at a time between the components. The bits follow one another in a series to form what are called characters. A parallel interface does the same thing except that the information goes over separate wires simultaneously and is then decoded.

Finally a computer graphics system must produce an image on paper or film. This is called *hard copy.* There are many kinds of printers and plotters that accomplish this and the image may be of any quality from coarse to smooth. Some computers use devices that operate much like an ordinary camera does to photographically reproduce the image from an internal screen.

When all the components are assembled the setup is called a computer graphics *workstation.* A typical workstation includes a personal computer, or PC; a chassis, or electronic expansion board for the PC; graphics software packages; a keyboard and drawing or tracing devices; a video output camera; a color display monitor; and a hard-copy printer.

This workstation by Geobased Systems includes a high-resolution monitor screen, a digitizing table with a sixteen-button tracing cursor, a floppy disk drive, more than one megabyte of memory, and linkage to a host computer with keyboard and mouse.

GRAPHICS TERMINALS

Computer-screen images are generated in several ways. One uses what is called a vector drawing terminal. The electron beam is directed from any point on the screen to any other point on the screen to create a pattern. The screen phosphors glow for only a short time, so the cathode-ray gun retraces, or refreshes, the path of the beam on the screen to keep it constantly visible. Since the image quickly disappears, it can also easily be redrawn in new positions. Thus the pictures can be moved or even animated.

A second system uses the *raster* principle. The word raster means "rake." This describes the way an electron beam can rake or sweep the viewing screen to create the image. The raster system takes advantage of the fact that the screen phosphors are arranged in horizontal lines stacked up to fill the picture area. To scan the entire screen the electron beam starts in the upper left corner and sweeps across line one. The beam then snaps back to the left and sweeps line two. It follows this zig-zag path until all lines are scanned and the beam ends in the lower right corner. Then the beam jumps back to the upper left corner and repeats

A raster scan traces horizontal lines from left to right and from top to bottom. The electron beam is blanked out when shifting between lines and when returning from lower right to upper left to start a new scan.

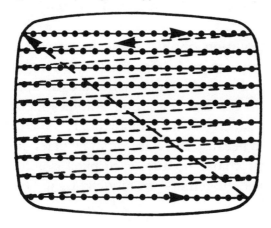

the whole process—perhaps sixty times each second. Although the beam is aimed along the path continuously, the electron stream is only turned on when particular pixels need to glow as part of the image to be generated.

A display screen can be operated in several "modes," or methods of display. These include the text mode, the low-resolution graphics mode, and the high-resolution graphics mode.

Suppose the screen is the same as a standard black-and-white TV screen. It is then made up of 480 visible lines, with perhaps 360 pixels in each line. Imagine that the screen is to be used in text mode. The screen might then be divided into rectangles nine dots wide and twelve dots high for the characters, with one extra dot as a horizontal spacer. On sophisticated systems the rectangles can vary in width according to the proportions of individual letters. In either case each rectangle of dots is used to form an alphabet character. Since the number of dots for each character is small, the letters have the typical jagged look of "computer" print.

In low-resolution graphics mode the screen is also divided into a rectangular grid. Suppose the rectangles are seven dots wide and four dots high with no extra space between rectangles. In the low-resolution graphics mode each rectangle is considered a unit, or pixel. The picture image is easy to build because there are very few pixel units. But the image is very coarse because each pixel is actually several dots clumped together—twenty-eight, in the example above.

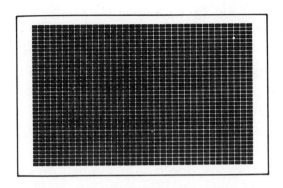

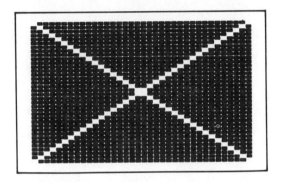

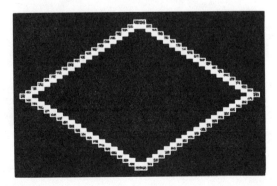

Display with very low-resolution "superpixels" enables beginners to use simplified graphic coordinates.

When the same screen is switched to high-resolution graphics mode, each dot—rather than each rectangle—is used as a pixel. Then the quality of the picture is as high as the total capability of the screen. Individual pixels are numbered from left to right and also from top to bottom. These horizontal and vertical number pairs are called *co-ordinates*. They are stored as bits in the computer memory.

A screen like that used for commercial television provides a picture image that is barely adequate for graphics. Most computer graphics screens have a greater number of lines and pixels. For example, a modest computer graphics display screen may use 640 pixels per line and 480 horizontal scan lines for a total of 307,200 pixels illuminating the screen area. More sophisticated units use 1,024 pixels per line with 780 scan lines for a total of almost 800,000 pixels.

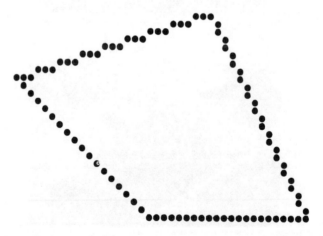

In a raster display, angled lines can generate groups of "stepped" pixels, creating typical jagged lines.

Screens using full color may have a resolution of up to 2,000 × 2,000 color pixel groups. And some very high-resolution computer graphics systems displaying a single color use a square screen with 4,096 horizontal pixels and 4,096 scan lines to yield a total of nearly 17 million pixels over the entire screen area.

☐ COLOR AND BLACK AND WHITE ☐

Screens that display only one color are called monochrome. "Mono" means one and "chrome" means color. On a monochrome screen, phosphors glow in only a single color. Typical choices are green, amber (yellow-orange), or white. Normally each color glows brightly against the darker background of the screen. Whichever color the system is designed for, that color only appears on the screen.

For full-color effects the arrangement of screen phosphors is more complex. Phosphors must be present that glow separately in the colors red, blue, and green. These are the three primary colors of projected light. They are called additive primaries. Blue and red light together produce a slightly purplish red called magenta. Blue and green produce a slightly greenish blue called cyan. And red and green light, surprisingly, produce yellow. When all three additive primaries are combined, the result is white light. And when all three are absent, the effect on the viewing screen is black. Thus, with only red, blue, and green phosphors, all possible color blends and variations can be achieved.

It is possible to activate several colors with only one

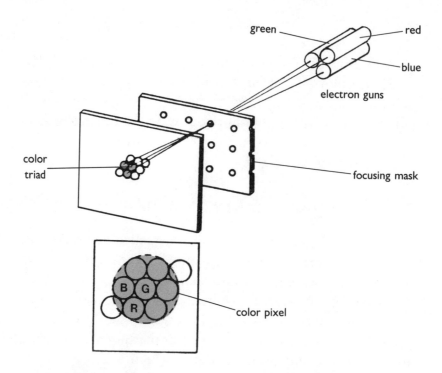

A color CRT tube with three electron guns. One stimulates blue phosphors, the second stimulates green, and the third stimulates red. Phosphors are arranged in repeated triads on the screen. A cluster of seven phosphors equals one color pixel.

Sony Trinitron® doubles the number of dots per line for color TV, improving graphic resolution.
Top: Standard color "pitch," or line count.
Bottom: Trinitron super-fine pitch.

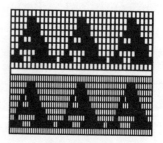

electron gun if the different colors of screen phosphors respond to different intensities of electron flow. The beam can then shift rapidly among the three separate intensities to stimulate one set of phosphors to glow red, another set to glow blue, and still a third set to glow green.

Usually, however, three electron guns are used to generate the three primary colors of projected light. The guns are clustered in a triad. Their projected beams cross at tiny holes spaced in even rows in a focusing mask behind the display screen. The beams stimulate corresponding triads of red, blue, and green phosphors on the screen. A cluster of seven color phosphors is considered one color pixel.

A slightly different system uses vertical slots in an "aperture grill" to allow more electrons to reach the screen. Using aperture grill focusing and a single color gun, Sony® has developed a color image in which the number of units per line appears doubled, giving improved resolution and greater detail.

☐　　　COMPUTER LANGUAGES　　　☐

At the most fundamental level computers work by means of electrical codes. These handle a variety of commands and functions that can be called *languages*. Computer languages allow people to "talk" to computers and computers to communicate with each other. These language codes work at different levels and for different purposes. They are essential for generating any image on the computer display screen, and they fall into three categories: machine code, assembler languages, and high-level languages.

The *machine code* is the binary code that a computer understands—the 1's and 0's that build essential bits and bytes of information. It is the most basic code or program that the computer uses.

Every computer also has its own assembler language. This involves two- or three-letter "words" that cover specific instructions, such as where in the computer memory to store a certain number.

High-level languages are the common user languages. These use English words or abbreviations. For instance, in one language, the command RUN tells the computer to start a program. Examples of high-level languages are FOR-TRAN, BASIC, and Pascal. Each of these has its own characteristics. FORTRAN, short for "*for*mula *trans*lation," is often used by engineers because it is good for mathematical calculations. FORTRAN is called a compiled language because it works through another program or *compiler* that reads all of the FORTRAN statements. The compiler converts them to machine code in order to set them in the best sequence for the computer to process.

BASIC is an acronym for "*B*eginner's *A*ll-purpose *S*ymbolic *I*nstruction Code." It is usually a noncompiled language. If so, it is slower because each line of language code is changed to a machine code command before the next line can be processed. The language called Pascal, named for a French philosopher and mathematician, was developed as an improvement on both FORTRAN and BASIC.

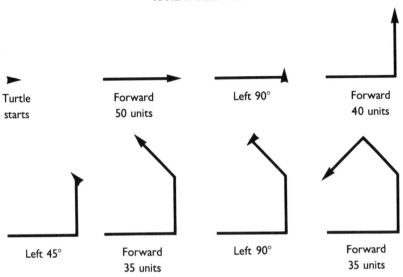

Constructing a computer image of a house with "turtle" geometry. The command FORWARD moves the turtle (arrowhead) a desired number of screen units in the direction it is facing. Commands LEFT and RIGHT rotate the arrowhead the desired number of degrees. A series of such procedures builds a "program" or "function" that can be stored in computer memory.

Most computer graphics systems require special pro-grams called *functions* and *subroutines*. A function is a simple task like computing the angle between two lines that meet. A group of related functions can be combined into a subroutine. For instance, a computer graphics subroutine might handle all the steps in drawing the sides of a triangle, rectangle, or other polygon. Collections of functions and subroutines are called libraries. These programs are "built in" to enable the computer to repeat specific image-making tasks quickly again and again.

2

BUILDING COMPUTER IMAGES

In order for an image to appear on the display screen, a computer must have a control device. The most basic of these is the keyboard. The standard version is called a QWERTY keyboard, after the arrangement of letters in the third row of keys. Above this row are the numbers 1 through 0, which also carry special characters available with the shift key. The QWERTY system was developed for the typewriter in the 1800s to distribute commonly used characters over the whole keyboard. This way typewriter mechanisms would not jam up with fast use. The system has remained the standard ever since.

Most computers use a version of the QWERTY keyboard that has additional keys at the left and right. At the left or above may be a set of function keys labeled F1 through F10 or perhaps F15. These control particular computer commands. At the right there is usually a set of nine keys grouped in a square. These look like numbers on a push-button phone, although number arrangements vary. The number keys contain other designations as well, used with the shift key. These include Page Up and Page Down, commands used to advance to a new page on the screen or to return to a previous page; arrows pointing to left and right and up and down; and the special functions marked End and Home. These numbered and coded keys can control the movements of a *cursor* across the screen. This is a tiny target

The MAC-101 keyboard by DataDesk includes a standard QWERTY keyboard, function keys, page controls, cursor controls, and a separate numeric keypad.

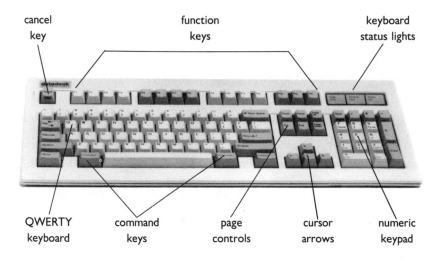

cancel key · function keys · keyboard status lights

QWERTY keyboard · command keys · page controls · cursor arrows · numeric keypad

cross or flashing square that moves elements into place or is used to build and edit lines and shapes on the screen. The standard line return key may be used to enter computer commands, and a back-space key may be used to erase mistakes. Some keyboards are very compact. Others offer divided sections. No two computer keyboards are exactly alike, but the functions and commands are often similar and are easily learned.

Next to the basic keyboard the *mouse* is one of the most common control devices used in computer graphics. It contains a roller ball that moves easily across a flat surface. Movements of the mouse are duplicated by a cursor on the computer screen. A mouse can be used to draw lines, to point, and to circle objects to be moved, transposed, or edited. Once the command has been selected on the screen, the click of a button on the mouse activates it.

A mouse can be constructed in several different ways. Most are mechanical, with the ball type being the most common. Gentle pressure on the mouse creates friction between the ball and a flat surface. The surface is usually a tabletop, but it can also be a friction pad designed for tighter contact. As the mouse is dragged along, the ball rotates in any direction. This rotating motion is transferred to two pressure rollers in contact with the ball. The rollers are set at right angles to each other. One roller picks up horizontal rotations of the ball; the other picks up vertical rotations. Rods connect the rollers to rotating disks. Points on the disks rotate past an electrical contact bar—or sometimes slots in the disk allow light to pass through to be

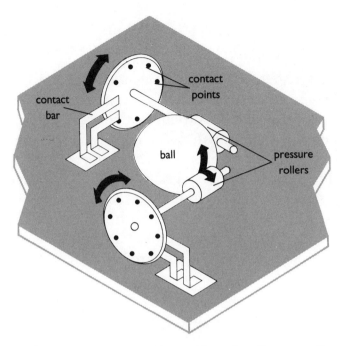

A mechanical mouse. The ball rolls on a table surface. Pressure rollers turn horizontal and vertical disks so points pass electrical contacts. Signals are translated to cursor movements on the computer screen.

detected by a phototransistor. In either case, coded electrical signals pass through a cord to the computer. There they are translated into cursor movements on the screen that are horizontal, vertical, or any blend of the two, resulting in all possible combinations.

Another type of mechanical mouse uses two plastic wheels set at right angles to each other. Still another variety has no moving parts at all but works with light of two different colors. The light beams are reflected from a pad with a special grid of black and blue lines that cross each other. One color represents motion along a horizontal axis; the other represents motion along a vertical axis.

A mouse will also have from one to three control buttons that can be pushed in various patterns to command the computer. A mouse with one button is simplest but will require a repeated number of clicks to initiate certain commands. A two-button mouse is usually convenient for professionals, who may use many different types of programs. With this type you can press the left button, the right button, or both at the same time. Mice with three buttons are even more flexible but also are harder for most people to learn to use.

Although the mouse was popularized by Apple® Computer, it has been imitated in slightly different versions

This three-button mouse offers seven different control combinations.

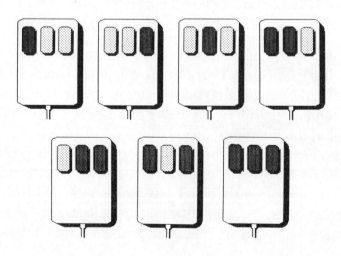

The Turbo Mouse has optical sensors that respond to finger touch on a gyroscopic ball. Rapid motion causes the cursor to jump across the screen. Slow motion "fine tunes" the cursor position.

throughout the computer industry. A company called Kensington Microware has developed an improvement called Turbo Mouse®. It is quicker and easier to use than the standard Apple mouse. Instead of being dragged along to cause the ball inside to roll, the unit is fixed and only the ball is moved. When the ball is moved rapidly, the cursor jumps to a distant position on the screen. When it is moved slowly, the unit fine-tunes the cursor for detailed work. A single function button is duplicated both to the left and to the right of the ball. The buttons can be used interchangeably. The ball rotates gyroscopically and four optical sensors within the unit respond accurately to the smallest movement.

Still another way of creating an image on the computer screen is with a tablet and stylus. A graphics tablet looks like a drawing board and works in a similar way. Tablets vary in size from desktop models to ones that measure five feet by three feet, the size of a professional drafting table. The artist uses a stylus or "pen" that looks much like a regular writing tool. The stylus may actually make a mark on paper fastened to the tablet. Or it may simply be moved across the surface. Either way, a sensor in the tablet tracks the motions of the stylus and translates them into lines, brush strokes, or shading on the screen, much as would be done by hand. Since the tablets store binary information, or digits, they are called digitizing tablets.

A sketch tablet. A "drawing" pen transmits an electronic or magnetic signal to a receiving grid under the tablet surface. The point of strongest signal is measured as the crossing of horizontal and vertical grid lines, giving the coordinate location of the pen point.

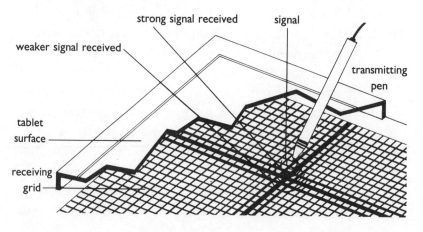

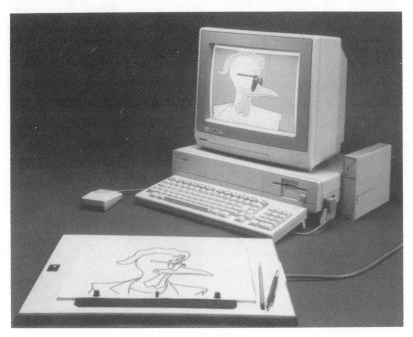

The Easyl® by Anakin allows the use of a pad and pencil in place of a mouse to draw images that appear on the screen of an Amiga computer.

Tablets require one of three pointing devices: a stylus, a pen, or a cursor. The stylus and pen are the most popular. The stylus has a blunt point and is used either to follow the lines of something already drawn or to draw freehand on the tablet. The pen does the same thing but also has an ink cartridge and a ball point. Therefore it can be used to make a fresh drawing on blank paper fastened to the surface of the tablet. The cursor looks something like a mouse but has a lens opening with a cross-hair target. By looking through the magnifying lens the artist can use the cross hairs to trace the lines of a drawing. This triggers the computer to direct a cursor in the same path across the screen.

A cursor with cross hairs for tracing is provided with the CalComp® 2500 digitizing tablet.

The motion of the control stylus is detected in several different ways. The most common is the antenna-transmitter method. Beneath the tablet surface is a grid of fine wires. The stylus point transmits an electronic signal to the grid. The horizontal and vertical wires receiving the strongest signals trigger the control circuitry to respond to a numbered position on the "x" or vertical axis and the "y" or horizontal axis. The coordinate point is then reproduced on the grid of the video screen.

Another sensing method is called resistive touch. In this system there is a narrow space between layers of the tablet. Stylus pressure causes the uppermost layer to touch the one below at that particular point, and a current flows between the layers.

A third method uses high-frequency sound. Ultrasonic waves are transmitted from the pen tip and are picked up by two bar microphones joined in an "L" shape around two sides of the drawing area. The ultrasounds cannot be heard. An advantage of this method is that no special tablet is needed. Any convenient surface can become the drawing area. The coordinate location of the pen point is determined by comparing the signal strength at each microphone, rather like a radio direction-finding system works.

Most tablets can also substitute for a keyboard. Typically there is a list or "menu" of symbols along one edge of the tablet. Sometimes a menu may flash up on the video screen. When the stylus or the cursor touches a menu symbol, the computer is commanded to follow a certain function or to place something into memory.

A variation of the stylus is a pointing instrument called the light pen. When the point of the pen is held against the video screen itself, it interacts with the computer coordinates at that point. In this way drawings or corrections can be made directly on the viewing screen. The light pen interacts directly with the electron beam inside the video screen. The pen point holds a lens system and a photodetector. When the pen detects the electron scanning beam, it emits an electronic pulse. The pulse goes through a cord from the pen to the computer's CRT *controller*. The controller calculates the pen position by measuring the time between the start of the CRT scanning beam and the time it reaches the pen point and computes the correct coordinate point on the screen. When the light pen is pressed against the screen,

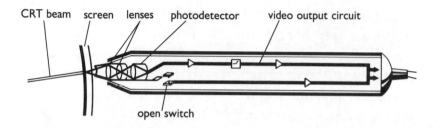

CRT beam   screen   lenses   photodetector   video output circuit

open switch

Above: An electron beam passes through the lenses of a light pen. A photodetector emits an electronic pulse. A CRT controller calculates the position
on the screen and a cursor follows the pen tip.
Below: A light pen is pressed against the screen to make a menu selection.
A switch closes and the pen sends an "enter" command.

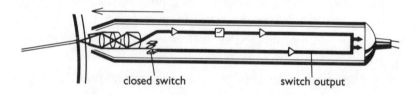

closed switch   switch output

that point is then entered into the computer as part of a
line that is being drawn or altered. It is more awkward to
draw on the video screen than on a flat tabletop and a
connecting cord has to be dragged along with the pen. However, new cordless models are being developed that may be
more flexible and easier to use.

As a simplified variation a finger is substituted for the
light pen. In this case a transparent plastic "sandwich"
placed over the display screen is sensitive to the touch and
location of a fingertip. IBM® has gone a step further with
Infoscreen, in which resistive touch is built directly into the
display itself.

PICTURE SCANNERS

Sometimes a completed drawing or photograph needs to be transferred to the screen. This can be done with a process called scanning. With drawing tablets, pens, and digitizing cursors, lines must be traced by hand to create the image. By comparison, scanners work automatically.

Suppose a drawing is to be transferred to the screen. This can be done in two ways. With a desktop or sheetfed scanner, the drawing itself is fed into the scanner, which scrolls it past a narrow slot. Light reflected from the drawing goes through a prism and lens unit to strike a charged-coupled

Artwork passes through a sheetfed scanner. Light is reflected from the paper surface through a slot. The lens and prism focus the image detail onto a charged-coupled device line by line.

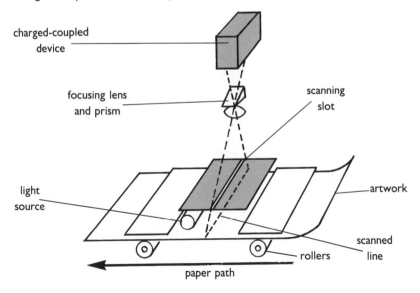

device, or CCD, that converts light impulses to electrical signals. This allows the image to be digitized or mapped line by line.

With the second method a flatbed scanner is used. A camera focuses the image of a whole page onto a photodiode array or scanning element. This sends information to a scanner controller that digitizes it to form what is called a bit map. However it is captured, the scanned picture information can be stored on floppy disk to be reproduced at any time.

A feature called "optical character recognition," or OCR, is built into some scanners. During scanning, printed alphabet characters are compared with characters stored in computer memory. When matching occurs, the computer "recognizes" words and sentences, which can then be stored directly on floppy disk.

Scanning a photograph is a more difficult task than scanning a drawing. Even a black and white photograph has an almost unlimited number of shades of gray, ranging from very light through medium to deep grays that are almost black. In the photograph, transitions from one level of gray to another are smooth and continuous. The photo is said to have "continuous tone."

When photographs are reproduced in newspapers and magazines the gray shades are translated into tiny dots of regular spacing but varying size. In a newspaper there may be from 85 to 100 of these dots per inch. In books and fine glossy publications there can be 133, 150, or even 200 dots

A photo of a tiger scanned and digitized for an Apple computer, available with MAC Hypercard® software.

per inch. When the dot count is high, the dots become so tiny that to the eye and brain there is the illusion of smooth tones.

Computer printers also represent tones as combinations of lines or dots. The larger the dots, the more grainy the image appears. The finer the dots, the smoother and more detailed the image. Until recently, most standard computers could store information about only a few shades of gray, and printers generated images with very obvious lines or dots.

However, a new generation of equipment is making it possible to scan, store, and print computer images with a much cleaner look. Part of the solution is in special gray-scale or gray-level scanners. For example, an 8-bit scanner

Top: A photo converted to 100 halftone dots per inch for conventional printing. All shades of gray are represented.
Center: The same photo scanned with a four-bit Abaton gray-scale machine. There are 50 dots per inch and only 16 levels of gray.
Bottom: The same photo processed with an eight-bit Datacopy scanner and printed by a Linotronic® 300 laser printer. There are 100 dots per inch and 256 levels of gray.

stores eight binary numbers for each pixel area sampled in a photograph. Such a scanner stores a total of 256 gray values, the number two multiplied by itself eight times.

The number of gray levels in the hard-copy output depends on the resolution of the printer. It may handle anywhere from only four up to a very smooth-looking 64 or even 256 gray levels, the maximum held by the scanner.

◻ **ALPHABET SHAPES AND STYLES** ◻

More and more, the human element is being programmed into computer graphics. A company called Inscribe has developed a way of using a computer to do the kind of beautiful handwriting called calligraphy. In calligraphy an artist uses a pen with a chisel-shaped point. When the pen is held at a constant angle, the lettering appears with both thick and thin strokes as the letter shapes are formed.

The Inscribe system uses letter forms held in computer memory. These are spaced or linked to build words on the video screen. The computer then commands a special Japanese-

made lettering bed that holds a calligraphic pen. The machine works as a plotter in which the usual round-tip pen is exchanged for the artist's pen.

A job that might take a handwriting artist ten hours to

Above: The plotter pen system by Inscribe "draws" hand lettering by automatic computer command.

Below: A sample of Inscribe lettering.

CELEBRATE AMERICA!

JOIN US ON THE 4TH OF JULY
FOR A BARBEQUE

design can be finished in less than ten minutes on the computer. At first, customers complained that the computer writing looked too perfect, so the designers programmed uneven brush strokes and other slight imperfections into the system. This way the lettering takes on a partly accidental or human look. The White House now uses the Inscribe system to send out notes and cards that need to look as if they were lettered by hand.

Some computer software offers a selection of typefaces, called fonts. Font is simply a term for all the characters of a particular alphabet design including capital letters, small letters, punctuation marks, and mathematical or other special symbols.

One typestyle package is MacIkarus, made by a company called Ikarus. This software package has 1,563 fonts of type. Furthermore it has a unique editing system for those who want to design their own typestyles. You can start with any preselected font, perhaps an ornate style with a hand-drawn look. First, flash the capital letter *A* on the screen. The letter form will fill the whole screen. Small notch marks automatically appear spaced along the lines and curves of the letter shape. Using a mouse, the screen cursor can be shifted to any of the marks and used to push or pull the line in any direction. By dragging parts of the line sideways, the letter *A* can take on a somewhat different shape. The change can be small or great; it is up to the artist. Any new or modified creations can then be stored just like the other fonts held in memory. With MacIkarus letter forms can be enlarged, reduced, made to tilt or appear italic, made narrower (con-

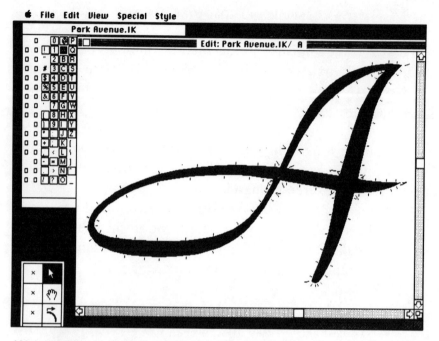

With MacIkarus software, the shape of an alphabet character can be changed by pushing or pulling "bandles" spaced along the outlines.

densed) or wider (expanded), outlined, shaded in, or shadowed. The software is simple enough for an amateur but flexible enough for professional designers.

☐   **HARD-COPY IMAGES**   ☐

Whatever design is created on the computer graphics screen eventually needs to be printed as hard copy. This means that the image will come out either on paper or on film from a camera.

To produce a hard-copy image on paper a machine called

a plotter or a printer can be used. There are several kinds. In a pen plotter a pen moves in only two directions representing the horizontal and vertical axes. If the paper is stationary, as in a bed or frame, the device is called a flatbed plotter. Plotter pens can be of interchangeable line widths. Sometimes a fixed line is retraced next to itself to build a wider line. Felt tip, ball-point, or liquid ink pens are all used. The paper is held by grippers or by vacuum suction.

In a pen plotter all curved lines are typically generated from a series of very short horizontal lines and appear stacked or "stepped." These steps range in resolution from a coarse .002 inches to a much less noticeable .0005 inches in size.

Plotters from Houston Instrument.
Left: The Flatbed DMP-29 uses a single pen with eight interchangeable colors.
Right: The PC Plotter 695A uses roller feed and a four-color pen carousel.

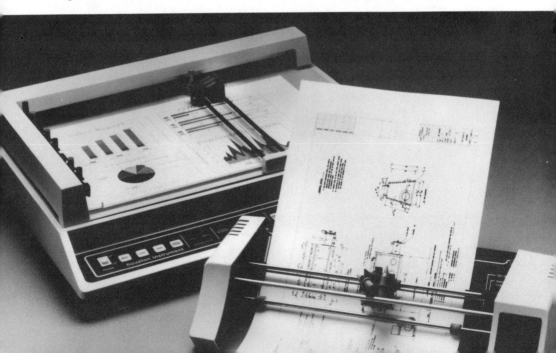

A drum plotter is a variation of the pen plotter. With this type the pen moves only left and right in the horizontal axis while a rotating drum feeds the paper past it. Paper rolls range from about eight or ten inches wide up to six feet wide, for reproducing engineering drawings. The paper roll can run continuously with sheets torn off as needed. A drum plotter uses either a stepped motor or a servomotor. The size of the step determines the degree of resolution from one horizontal line to the next.

On a plotter the pen tip can be changed manually to vary the thickness or the color of the line. Plotters may use a single color or up to eight or ten pens for a wide variety of colors. On some plotters the machine itself can automatically change pens. A disadvantage of the plotters is that pen points or tips can wear down or run out of ink.

The drafting plotter from Houston Instrument handles a six-pen changer and reproduces computer drawings on a 36-inch by 48-inch sheet.

Many computer plotters use a raster principle, producing the page by means of scanned and closely spaced horizontal lines. Raster plotters are of several varieties. One is the electrostatic. This works like a common photocopying machine but uses paper that is coated. The image-producing unit consists of a horizontal row of "brushes," or metallic nibs, spaced only about .125 millimeters apart. The nibs correspond to pixels on a video screen. A scanner determines which nibs in any row will be part of the picture image. These are given an electric charge that is transferred to the coated paper. Thus the complete image is laid down electrically, line by line. The charged paper then passes through a bath of ink or toner. The toner is attracted only to the tiny points on the page that carry an electrical charge. The paper may accept black toner only, or toners of several colors. Then the paper must run through the scanning process once for each color. Combining the three primary colors used in printing (magenta, cyan, and yellow) can produce overlapped combinations that represent a full-color painting or photograph.

The thermal plotter is similar to the electrostatic plotter. In this case the paper is heat-sensitive. A sheet of special paper that holds ink in a wax layer is placed between the paper to be printed on and a row of tiny brush points. Heat from the brushes melts the wax, releasing microscopic capsules of ink onto the paper. A thermal plotter can also handle color reproductions with separate passes of the paper.

Another raster plotter is the dot-matrix printer. This has a print head consisting of a matrix of tiny tubes. Each tube

Above: The Versatec narrow-format electrostatic plotter/printer produces high-quality black-and-white or color copies.

Below: A closeup of the Versatec wide-format plotter/printer.

contains a tiny wire. An ink ribbon passes between the print head and the paper. As the head passes across a line at high speed, selected wires project from the tubes to impress the desired pattern onto the paper. The miniature matrix head may print a vertical row of nine dots, for example. To reproduce a typewriter-style character, the print head shifts or scans to generate a grid, and combinations of the grid dots form the alphabet letter. The dots actually appear as dashed lines, giving the printout its typical jagged "computer" look. Graphic images of lines and circles or other shapes are all formed from the tiny dashed lines. Sometimes the machine can be adjusted to provide either a fast printout with medium resolution or a slow printout with tighter detail in the spacing of the matrix dots on the page. The choice is often a compromise between the two.

Left: A perfect alphabet character.
Center: The character made by bit-mapping on a computer text matrix.
Right: The character improved by computerizing conic, or "C," curves to make the shape more accurate.

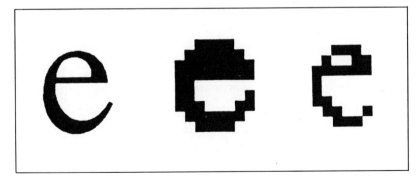

Some dot-matrix printers have increased the number of pins in the vertical row from nine to twenty-four. Spacing is controlled by the horizontal jumps of the matrix row, and rows are interlocked by advancing the paper only one-half dot space at a time. Newer models are quieter than before, making less noise than a daisy-wheel typewriter printer. Speed has also been dramatically improved. Only ten to twenty-five seconds are now needed to print an entire page of information. And the high-resolution head brings a much smoother look to drawings and photographic materials as well as to the alphabet characters of typefaces.

A further improvement can be made with a computer that stores sets of mathematical curves. When the curves are applied to alphabet characters, their shapes become more exact and can then be more accurately reproduced by the printer.

The ink-jet printer uses a principle of electrostatic attraction similar to that employed by a photocopy machine. A carriage rapidly traverses the blank page line by line as tiny droplets of colored ink are propelled onto the paper. Typical resolution is very good, with only from four to six dots per millimeter.

Still one more raster printer that is rapidly growing in popularity is the laser printer. A laser directs a finely focused beam of light of pure color, or frequency, and high intensity. Where the beam strikes a rotating drum, an electrostatic charge is generated. The drum attracts ink toner which is transferred to a sheet of paper, producing a visible dot.

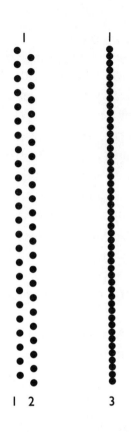

Left to right: Column 1 shows the imprint of a vertical dot-matrix head with 24 pins.
Column 2 shows the same head imprint shifted down one-half dot space.
Column 3 shows imprints 1 and 2 overlapped by the printer, doubling the dot count for greater density and detail.

1 2   3

Left: A greatly magnified halftone dot, like those used to reproduce photographs in books.
Center and right: Matrix patterns used by computer printers to represent the dot. The 4 by 4 patterns represent the round dot crudely. The 8 by 8 matrix represents the dot more accurately.

Current laser printers have a resolution of about 300 dots per inch, good enough to reproduce drawings and type characters with a reasonably smooth look. However, technical advances are bringing laser printers that will have a resolution of around 1,000 dots per inch and greater. With these the look of the printed page can be almost as smooth as an original photograph.

Some printers and plotters are designed to generate images in full color. These devices normally require a separate pass for each of the three printer's primary colors plus a fourth pass for the color black. If the printer is a dot-matrix type, the ink ribbon may have bands of separate colors much like a two-color typewriter ribbon.

Of course if the page information consists only of type characters, an electronic typewriter can be connected to the computer to automatically type out the page at high speed. Such a printer, however, can produce only crude pictures; it can only type an organized pattern of characters, such as the letter X, across the page.

A different way of getting a hard-copy version of a computer image is to use camera and film. One such professional computer typesetter is made by the Compugraphic Company. A keyboard is used to set up words, columns, borders, and boxes on a computer screen. The digital information is then translated into holes punched on a roll of tape. The tape is fed into a camera unit that uses lenses and film negatives of the various type fonts and symbols available for the system. Computer commands trigger the machine to select the correct type font and enlarge or reduce it to the correct size. The output of the machine is a clear image developed on photographic paper.

One can take a direct photograph of a computer screen with an ordinary camera. However, reflections cause problems and the contrast may not be very good. Furthermore, straight lines may appear bent because of the curvature of the screen. The solution is a unit with an internal camera and screen. Suppose a high-resolution image has already been produced on a computer system. It may have been drawn with a tablet and stylus, or it may have been developed from a scanned photograph or drawing. The final result appears on an internal display screen. This screen has a perfectly flat surface so there is no distortion. An internal camera focuses on the screen and a film negative and print are made in the usual way. The smoothness of the photograph depends on the resolution of the computer system. With high-quality systems the result can be as good as an ordinary glossy photographic print.

If the image is in color, three separate exposures are made by the internal camera. A color filter is used for each of the primary colors of light: red, green, and blue. The internal screen is black and white. It receives each color image separately. The projected light passes through the appropriate color filter on its way to the camera and photographic film. The developed film image can be of excellent color quality and contrast.

$$\boxed{3}$$

COMPUTER GRAPHICS
AT WORK

☐   **PICTURES FOR COMMUNICATIONS**   ☐

Many software packages are on the market to help commercial artists prepare pictures with computer graphics. Such pictures may be drawings, cartoons, photographs, charts, or graphs that are to be seen in a variety of publications from newspapers and newsletters to magazines and books. A variety of graphics software packages have been designed for use on Apple computers such as the Mackintosh™ or "Mac," each with its own capabilities. One basic package used on the Macintosh is called MacDraw® and is available for home or office applications. It is useful for making simple maps and line drawings. A more flexible package is called Cricket Draw® and has somewhat more professional options. Cricket Draw relies on a computer language developed by Adobe® Systems that is called PostScript®. PostScript allows images to be conveyed to any output device that works on a raster principle. The dot resolution is limited only by the printer or plotter, a distinct advantage.

With Cricket Draw the artist can make lines, rectangles, and ovals. Objects can be moved, enlarged or reduced, and rotated one degree at a time. Outlined areas can be automatically filled with gray shading that shifts gradually from light to dark across the area. Lettering styles can be mixed together, and finished pages can be broken up into the halftone dots that are used for commercial printing.

A similar package for the Macintosh is Adobe Illustrator. This is a popular program for professional designers and illustrators. It is used for freehand drawing and also for converting existing images into screen graphics. For example, a scanner used with Adobe Illustrator can reproduce a photograph or a piece of artwork by a process called bitmapping. This step generates a "template" that appears on the screen. The artist then can use Adobe's pen tool to trace the template in lines and curves. A line can be stretched, shortened, or reshaped by dragging "anchor points" at the end of the line or "direction points" along the line. Segments can be removed or added to change the length of the line. And once a line encloses an area, that space can be filled with black, white, or a chosen shade of gray.

A software package called LaserPaint® goes even further. It has many of the capabilities of both Cricket Draw and Adobe Illustrator. It also lets the artist control eight full

With Deluxe Paint II a portion of the image is enlarged with zoom feature and a "gleam" is added to the owl's eye.

pages of space as a single unit. Formats can be planned with columns of text for brochures, magazines, or newspapers. Professional commands allow printer's spacings to be added between lines of type. Colors to be printed on top of one another can be aligned with special register marks. And markings can even be included to show where a page will be folded and cut after it is printed. A similar software package called PageMaker™ is produced by Aldus. Such packages combined with high-resolution printers now have created a new computer specialty called desktop publishing.

Computer graphics is increasingly being used in the newspaper industry. One example is the large syndicate called Knight-Ridder, which includes twenty-eight newspapers in the United States. Mac graphics software programs have been selected and developed for these newspapers to standardize art and charts and to save time in meeting daily deadlines.

Artist Richard Furno works with a large newspaper called

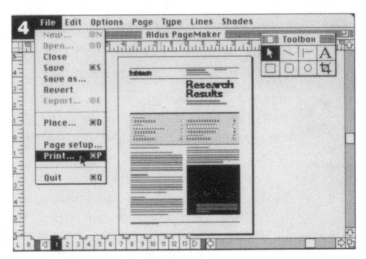

PageMaker by Aldus allows
a user to plan a page layout
for desktop publishing,
complete with typefaces
and graphic images.

the *Washington Post*. Furno invented his own software
package called Azimuth. It was first planned for the IBM
PC and later adapted for the Macintosh.

Azimuth is used to prepare a view of the earth from any
height or angle. The program can call up from computer
memory an image of a county, a state, an entire continent,
or even the earth as seen from outer space.

Mac software accessories called Sizer and Adjacency are
especially helpful to newspapers in making bar graphs. Say
the value of the U.S. dollar as it changes from month to
month is to be shown as a series of vertical bars of different

heights. *Adjacent* means "next to," and with Sizer and Adjacency, the computer can generate the bar images on the screen and mark off the correct height of each bar in relation to its neighbor. The information can be stored so that new figures can quickly be added without having to completely redraw the graphs each time.

Computerized graphics for newspapers must include boxes, borders, titles, labels, captions, columns of type, and many other elements. A system such as PageMaker™ shows on the screen the proportions of a series of pages, two pages together, or a single page for planning locations of all the elements. Boxes flashed on the screen show where the columns of type must fit and where the pictures will go above or between the columns. A column of words will appear on the page and will even wrap around a picture, changing the width of the column automatically.

Other software specializes in the choice of type that can be used, including weight and other details. Adobe software for the Mac is made for just such a job. Another software package for page and type design, called Ready-Set-Go, has been designed by Letraset, a company specializing in making press-on graphics of letters, numbers, and symbols for commercial artists.

One of the problems in handling art for publication is fitting it to the page in exactly the right size. If there are details in an illustration, the artist may want to work on the picture in a scaled-up version, reducing it later to fit the width of several news columns. Chris Carr, a student in the

Visual Communications School of Ohio University, has solved this problem. As a project for an advanced degree he designed a system called Amperage just for keeping track of the sizes and dimensions of illustrations and zooming them up or down from one proportion to another.

Artist George Rorick has worked out his own procedures for the *Detroit News*. Rorick is an illustrator and cartoonist who uses software for the Macintosh in flexible combinations. One of his assignments was to create a map of one of the U.S. space shuttle flights. An outline map of a large section of the earth had to carry a grid of latitude and longitude and the accurate path of the shuttle as it crossed oceans and continents. Rorick used photos of the shuttle to trace a line drawing. He enlarged it so the software could be used to choose lines of different thicknesses in the drawing. The finished artwork was then reduced to fit over a portion of the map. Finally overlays were prepared for adding shadow areas and background tones.

As techniques improve, more and more picture information can be stored by computer. For instance, Rorick now prepares weather maps in which the graphic information is transmitted electronically to the newspaper's production plant twenty-eight miles away. No artwork needs to be delivered or sent through the mail.

One problem in computer graphics is converting a photograph or painting with many hues of color and shades of gray into a line drawing. Line drawings are simple to handle as computer images. They are easy to fill in with color and

Art prepared for the *Detroit News* by George Rorick.

Above: An outline world map is generated.
Right: A drawing of a space shuttle is developed from photos.
Below: A grid, shuttle art, background tone, and printer marks are combined using computer graphics.

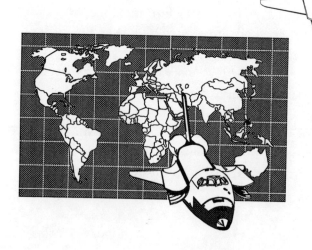

tones, and easy to exaggerate or alter in other ways.

The usual way of doing this is to trace the shapes in the photo or painting by hand. The photo is placed on a tablet and taped into place. A stylus pointer is then used to trace the desired outlines. This produces a line drawing on the computer screen. But an artist has had to take time and exercise skill in doing what amounts to practically an original drawing.

A new software program marketed by Silicon Beach Software has overcome some of these limitations. It is called Digital Darkroom. Darkroom has a feature called Auto-Trace. This lets the computer recognize basic shapes and the edges between them. The boundaries are converted to outlines and a simple line drawing takes the place of the

Digital Darkroom by Silicon Beach Software offers an automatic outlining feature called AutoTrace.

Top: A magnified straight line appears stepped where it crosses rows of pixels.
Center: The corrected line divides neighboring pixels into partial areas.
Bottom: Through "anti-aliasing" partial areas are converted to corresponding pixel densities. The eye is fooled and the line appears smooth.

picture's complicated tones and shadings. The software also can be used to adjust brightness and contrast of an image. It can use filters to blur, sharpen, or enhance edges between tone areas. And it can change or reorganize areas of gray with the touch of a "magic wand." For editing it can delete and add areas, or place selections in front of an existing image, behind the image, or even blended with the image.

Another high-quality graphics package has been developed by Truevision®. A maker of products such as the popular TARGA® and VISTA® for IBM personal computers, the company now also offers software for the Mac II. The graphics program is named NuVista®. It boasts ultra-high quality in both capturing and displaying images up to a pixel resolution of 1,024 × 768. The output signals provided by the new package are of broadcast quality.

A common problem even on some high-resolution screens is that diagonal lines still tend to look jagged at close viewing. The standard solution is to use a process called "anti-aliasing." Additional pixels bordering the lines are given varying densities, obscuring the jagged corners.

A new graphics terminal built by a company called Codonics has now removed this nuisance in another way. The Codonics 4096 has a basic screen count of 1,024 × 1,024 but cleverly uses multiple pixels of varying *sizes*. The effect is of a screen resolution of 16,000 × 12,000 units and the diagonal lines are truly smooth.

☐　　　　　IMAGE PROCESSING　　　　　☐

One special job done by computer is image processing. The original image might be on film and taken by an ordinary camera. It might be an infrared photograph taken at night using film sensitive to heat radiation. It might be a medical X ray. Or it might be an image broadcast back to earth from a spacecraft. Whatever the source, the image contains information or detail that needs to be sorted out or emphasized.

A computer can do this by converting the image into digital information. A grid is superimposed on the image. Scanners detect information about color and brightness for

Graphics terminal by Codonics uses new technology. Multiple pixels of varying sizes transform a 1,024 by 1,024 resolution screen to an apparent smoothness of 16,000 by 12,000. Enlargements show how jagged lines are eliminated.

each pixel unit. Color information will be separated into hue and brightness.

Once the information is digitally sorted, it can be processed in unique ways. A color hue can be made more intense or less intense. A chosen level of gray can be made darker or lighter. Or a particular kind of feature repeated throughout the picture can be given more contrast with surrounding tones.

An example of this was the processing of the first close-up pictures of the surface of Mars sent back by RCA cameras aboard the landing craft. The broadcast that reached the earth consisted of computerized bits of information. This was then reorganized so that shadows became deeper, colors appeared more descriptive of the planet's surface and atmosphere, and details of rocks and boulders seemed clearer. No new information was actually added. Instead, the existing information was *balanced* selectively to improve the quality of the picture. This balancing process depends on what is called "machine vision," a technical imitation of visual perception in the human eye and the process of pattern recognition in the human brain.

For a further example, suppose a set of numerical data is received from an earth-orbiting satellite. The digital data is rich in information. It can be transformed into a topographical chart that resembles a photograph. Formerly unexplored sections of the earth may become visible for the first time. Scientists can detect and measure the amounts of forested, cultivated, or snow-covered land, recognize rock and mineral formations and deposits, or even detect pollution in bodies of water. On the other hand, military agencies can search for weapons arsenals and troop installations by emphasizing shadows and enlarging selected areas. For each purpose different ratios or proportions among the stored numbers will yield pictures that emphasize what is important to the viewer.

This capability can be carried a step further by combining an industrial machine with cameras and computer processors. The result is robotics, a form of computer-aided manufacture, called CAM for short. Suppose a plant is making a part for a rocket engine. As the completed parts pass along an assembly line, each is examined by a computerized TV camera. The computer is programmed with a predetermined pattern so it can detect flaws in the shape, dimensions, or surface of the specialty part. When a part does not match the ideal image pattern, the computer triggers a robot arm to move down and lift the flawed part from the conveyor belt.

Image lines reversed from black to white with MAC Card Shoppe.

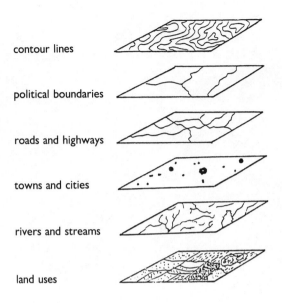

contour lines

political boundaries

roads and highways

towns and cities

rivers and streams

land uses

A computer graphics system can combine any number of overlays to create a map of a chosen region.

Many alterations can be made on a stored image. It can be rotated in position, reversed left to right, changed from a negative to a positive, enlarged or reduced, made narrower or wider or otherwise distorted in its dimensions, and highlighted or shadowed. Even part of the background or foreground can be artificially blurred so that it corresponds to changing depths of focus.

Image processing is extremely important to mapmakers, or cartographers. A computer can break down stored information into what are called data layers. A single section of geography can be separated into at least nine levels, including elevation contours, political boundaries, highways, land usage, railway networks, mathematical or geodetic

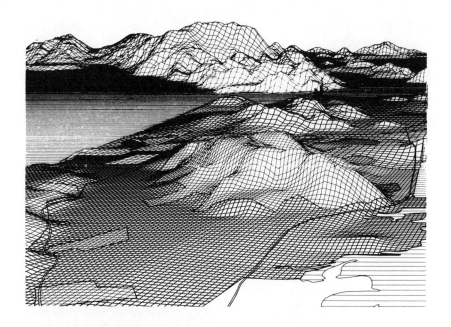

Above: A fishnet computer map of San Francisco Bay.

Below: A hillside mapped with contour lines by computer graphics.

data, towns and cities, drainage information, and place names. By combining selected layers many specialized maps can be developed, all from the same data bank.

One of the hardest tasks to computerize has been placing names on maps. This is a highly complex process. Names must not cover other important map details. They must fill certain areas even if there are no specific boundaries. They must vary in size, curve, and direction. And they must fall conveniently close to particular lines or points. Many of these placing problems have been solved by Herbert Freeman, a specialist in computer image processing at Rutgers University, who worked closely with John Ahn, a graduate student at Rensselaer Polytechnic Institute.

Freeman and Ahn reduced the tasks to "rules" that resembled the decisions made by an expert cartographer when adding place names to a map. The system is called Autonap, for *auto*matic *na*me *p*lacement.

The program starts with some specific computer rules. A feature name should span an entire area and match its overall shape. One and a half letter spaces should appear between the name and the boundaries at either end. Names that are not horizontal should always be curved. And horizontal names must be parallel with lines of latitude. Many similar rules are also programmed into the computer. Any of them may play a part in the computer's automatic decisions.

One use of automatic name placement involves the lines of latitude and longitude that appear on most maps. Lines of latitude circle the globe parallel to the equator. On maps of small areas they appear as straight lines, but on larger maps of continents they appear as curved lines. In the United States many state boundaries follow lines of latitude. Since most area names can be placed horizontally, their natural alignment is parallel to the lines of latitude. On a local map this is no problem for the computer. All latitude lines are horizontal, so all place names that fit remain horizontal like printed lines in a book.

But what if the latitude lines are curved? The computer first changes all curved latitude lines into horizontal lines. Then the place names are inserted between them so that lines and names are parallel. Finally, the curves of the latitude lines are restored and the place names automatically curve along with them. The result is natural alignment all across the map.

Or take an example of fitting a name to a state with an odd shape. Maryland is a typical challenge. In one section it is too narrow for any alphabet letters to be placed inside the boundaries, and in another section it is broken up by the shape of the waters of Chesapeake Bay. To find the best name placement the computer uses a "skeleton" principle.

The drawing at the top of page 65 shows the actual shape of Maryland. As a first step, the detailed wiggles of the boundaries are simplified to create a figure with straight-line edges. Each inside area is then mathematically divided by a center line. The shorter lines are automatically pruned away to leave one simple center line. The computer then smooths the line into a curve. Lastly, the alphabet letters are automatically placed so that half of each letter is above

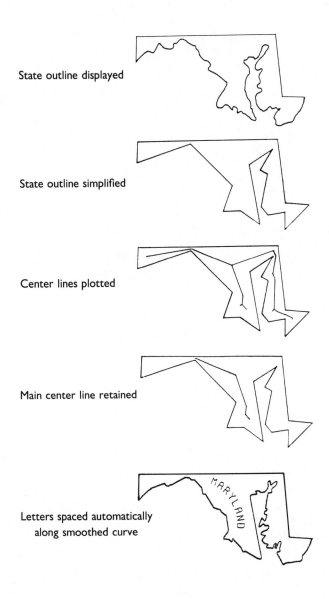

State outline displayed

State outline simplified

Center lines plotted

Main center line retained

Letters spaced automatically
along smoothed curve

The Autonap system labels Maryland automatically by computer.

and half is below the curved line. The name "MARYLAND" has been positioned by computer in the largest possible size and in a natural curve that is easy to read.

☐   COMPUTER-AIDED DESIGN   ☐

One of the fastest-growing applications of computer graphics is computer-aided design, or CAD for short. This is the use of detailed computer images for making drafting plans, scale drawings, and mechanical renderings of objects and structures. CAD is used by mechanical and civil engineers, lighting engineers, architects, and city planners. Machinery, automobiles, bridges, buildings, and towns are all designed on computers with CAD.

CAD must provide the same detail as a blueprint prepared with a slide rule and a T-square at a drafting table. Mathematical symbols and commands for linear and angular measurement must be programmed into the system. Objects need to be represented in a variety of views, all of which contain the same accurate information.

For this reason CAD systems differ from more basic computer graphics systems. In an inexpensive graphics program the computer may use whole numbers, or integers, to locate points on a display screen. These are converted to combinations of the binary digits 0 and 1. Lines are built on the screen from horizontal and vertical coordinates that represent the dots or pixels. These coordinate points work like a simple map or graph laid out on the screen. The coordinates are the only mathematical information describing the image.

CAD requires a much more sophisticated handling of object information. If only maplike coordinates were used, the stored numbers would soon become cumbersome to process. Instead, the CAD information describes the special characteristics of a line, including its location, size, angle of direction, any changing direction or curve, and its end points. Location can be fixed or flexible. The data are really a series of commands about *drawing* the line itself. With this type of representation, far more complex lines and curves can be conveniently stored digitally. These can be called up from computer memory at any time to reconstruct the line.

Since the binary information is related to commands about drawing a line, the number of screen coordinates available is irrelevant. The image can be drawn on a computer screen with low resolution or high resolution. When the image is enlarged, it simply becomes more detailed instead of coming out more coarse or ragged. And if it is printed out on a plotter with higher resolution than the video screen, the lines will appear as smoothly curved as the plotter will allow.

Computer-aided designs are usually prepared in several stages. Suppose an architect is designing a porch to attach to a house. He or she may want to correct some detail in a corner where a porch post rests on a metal plate. The solution is to use a computer "window." To create the window the designer circles that special corner area with a stylus on the CAD tablet, then presses a menu command on the tablet or draws a code symbol across the tablet. Say the code is a letter Z, for zoom up. When the Enter key is pressed, that section of the porch post is enlarged to fill the entire screen.

The designer may want to compare more than one area of the plan at the same time. Then several sections of the screen can be set aside as "viewports." Each viewport can hold its own particular detail of the overall plan for easy reference.

In CAD there is a need for computer commands that are characteristic of mechanical drawings. Lines may need to be dotted to show where they pass behind solid areas. A series of small curved lines may need to be set side by side to show where a bend occurs in a mechanical shape. Or drilled holes may need to be located very precisely, for example. For this purpose a center for the hole is located mathematically and a measurement is keyed for the diameter of the hole or its radius from center to edge. The hole will then automatically appear in the right place and the right size on the diagram. Arrows and numbers will need to be placed on the finished plan in order for a toolmaker or contractor to be able to actually construct the machine parts or building that is represented.

A CAD design starts with a related group of plan drawings. These are really three separate views of the modeled object. The first is a top view, the second a front view, and the third a side view. These are called orthographic views, from the term "ortho," meaning straight. It is like unfolding

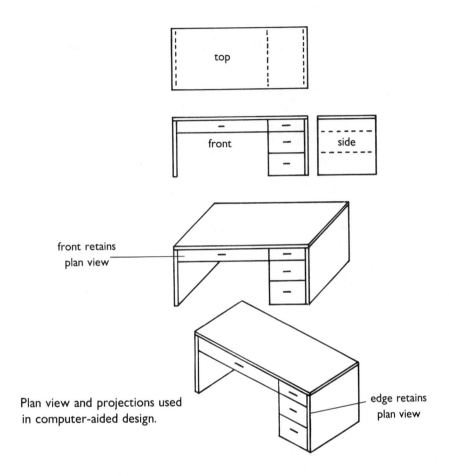

top

front

side

front retains
plan view

Plan view and projections used
in computer-aided design.

edge retains
plan view

the parts of a cardboard box so all can be seen at once.
When these drawings are completed on the computer screen,
the stored information can be used to construct several kinds
of perspective views.

3-D constructions of these views are called projections.
In one type of projection the front view stays the same as
the plan view, just as it was drawn flat on the viewing screen.

The top and side views are connected to the front but projected as if being viewed from above and to one side of the object. If the object is a desk, for example, the lines representing top and side are at an angle but parallel to each other.

In another type of projection, only the edge between the front and one side remains the same as it was drawn in the plan view. Front, sides, and top of the desk are all projected back at the same viewing angle.

As long as the plan view is complete, the computer can automatically generate a solid image of the object in the desired projection. The designer can also keep a transparent view of the object in which lines at the front overlap lines at the back. Some computer modeling systems can discard

Left: A CAD image showing all object lines.
Right: Hidden lines removed by computer.

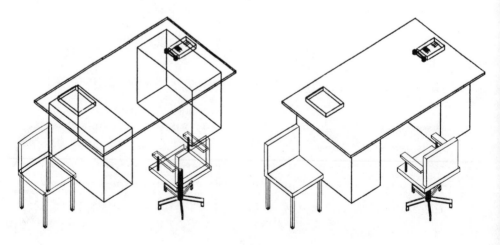

the "hidden" lines automatically. Once the object appears in 3-D, tones can easily be added to various surfaces to show parts that are in shade or away from a light source.

Many CAD systems have a viewing screen that is monochrome, showing typically green on black, for example. When the working drawing is printed out later, ink or plotter pen lines can be whatever color is desired.

Sometimes, however, a client wishes to see what a product will look like in natural color. Then a "red, green, blue," or RGB, system must be used as with a color TV. Areas of the drawing can be "painted." Such a system will also be able to render surfaces as dull or shiny and can even include several light sources and special reflections. Views can be rotated, tilted, and placed in any natural perspective and at any apparent distance from the observer. The computer will automatically add tints (degrees of white) and shades (degrees of black) to the colored surfaces as the views change.

CAD techniques are often used for commercial advertisements in magazines or on television. A common example is to convert a flat silhouette into a dramatically lit 3-D image that can be rotated in space. A CAD manufacturer called Cubicomp supplies software named Speedtrace with which this can be easily accomplished.

Suppose the original image is a group of alphabet initials. First the silhouette characters are automatically converted to an outline wireframe. The outlines are then "extruded" or pushed back to create three-dimensional depth. The new 3-D wireframe is then lighted, shaded, and completely rendered to look like a photograph of a solid model. The model

Speedtrace by Cubicomp converts a silhouette to outlines. Lines can then be "extruded" to generate a 3-D wireframe ready to be filled and shaded.

silhouette

wireframe

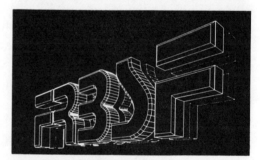

extruded wireframe

rendered model

can be seen from above, below, or even behind, and then rotated into the desired position. "Entertainment Tonight," the Olympic Games, and other TV broadcasts make use of such 3-D computer-aided design in their trademark images, or logos.

☐   **COLOR PRINTING**   ☐

Computer graphics is revolutionizing the printing industry. One of the most demanding jobs in printing is color separation. Let us say a color transparency is to be reproduced in an advertisement in a magazine. The color image must be separated into four printer's colors: magenta, cyan, yellow, and black. When these four ink colors are printed onto a page separately, they overlap and blend to re-create the effect of full color.

To accomplish this difficult task the color transparency is normally wrapped around a transparent drum. The drum is rotated while a focused laser light beam scans through the transparency in raster style. There is one scan to pick up the magenta color, another for the cyan, and so on. A film negative is made for each color. These are translated into transparent positive images that can be overlapped to see how the colors combine. Often the color is not accurate. Many adjustments and corrections have to be made to achieve a good copy of the original image. The corrected color negatives are used to photographically etch metal plates. Each plate, inked with its own color, makes a separate impression on the paper as it passes through the press, and the overlapped impressions reproduce the complete color image.

Today it is possible to handle the whole process through computer graphics. For example, the Scitex Company has developed an entire color separation system. The transparency is placed in a unit called a Smart Scanner. Artificial intelligence and microcomputer controls are used to analyze the color content of the transparency. The scanned image appears on the high-resolution color monitor. On the screen the image can be changed in almost any way possible. A color can be intensified in a chosen area. A section of the picture can be temporarily enlarged for detailed handwork, including changes made pixel by pixel. Something in the foreground of the picture can be dropped out and the background can be made to continue across the empty space. An object or person in the picture can be echoed or duplicated, or even reflected as if in a mirror. A second photo can overlap the first for a "ghosting" effect. Shadows can be put in with soft or sharp edges. Type and titles can be added in any color. An airbrushing tool can "spray" a fine mist of color more smoothly than could be done by any artist's hand. And the original scanned information, along with all steps and changes, can be stored digitally on reels of computer tape. Even years later, the original image and any altered stages can be called up with absolutely no loss of detail.

Once the color-corrected image is in final form, the computer can control equipment that chemically etches the metal plates that will be used to print the image on paper.

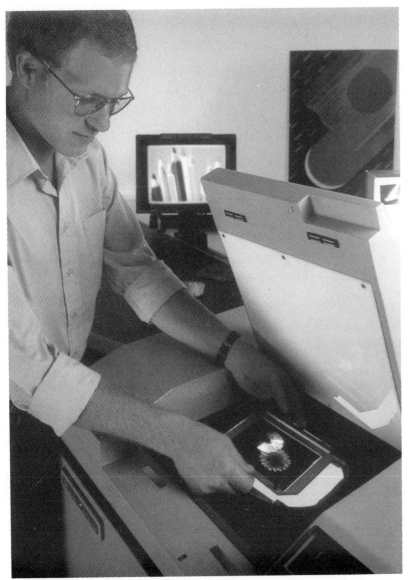

A technician places a transparency into the Scitex Smart Scanner, which automatically separates out the color information by computer.

Thus the usual photographic negatives are not needed. The entire process from image to printing plate can be accomplished by computer. A system like this may cost over a million dollars, but it can pay for itself with improvement in quality and the time and work saved on each color job.

☐　　　　　　**MUSIC GRAPHICS**　　　　　　☐

One of the most exciting uses of computer graphics is in composing music. Most personal computers now have software for both amateur and professional musicians. Music is composed on computer in two basic ways. With the first method, music staff lines appear on the screen. Notes and symbols are positioned with a mouse or stylus much as you would write directly on music manuscript paper. With the second method, an electronic keyboard is linked with the computer. Sounds played on the keyboard are stored in computer memory and are automatically translated into note symbols that appear on the screen. With either method, the music can be played back through the computer's own speaker or a stereo system. The music notation also can be turned into hard copy with a computer printer.

A quality music package is Concertware + MIDI 4.00, developed by Great Wave Software. With this system a chart of musical elements is called up on the video screen. From this the composer chooses the note and rest values that will be available throughout the composition. The computer's own alphabet keyboard or a MIDI (Musical Instrument Digital Interface) connected synthesizer can be used to perform the composition. The notes and rests of the performance are rounded off to the nearest values, and the pictured notation looks almost exactly like the music sounds.

In the Concertware system eight sound composites are assigned to eight musical staves. Each of these composites allows for up to eight "voices" per staff. Thus the composition can range from simple one- or two-hand keyboard music to a combo or orchestra of instrumental sounds.

The new Concertware package can be combined with another software package called Sonata, a PostScript music font made by Adobe. Notes, symbols, and staff lines produced by this font are not dependent on resolution. Therefore a good laser printer can be used for the final printout. And the printed image is close to the quality of published music.

The Concertware + MIDI 4.00 also handles lyrics for songs. When you press the tab key instead of the space bar, words and syllables are permanently attached to particular notes in the computer memory. Then if you change the note spacing, the word syllables automatically shift right along with the note placements.

A unique sound chip has been borrowed for the Apple IIGS® computer. It is the same electronic chip used in the Ensoniq Mirage synthesizer. By adding software, the GS can produce fifteen different voices of digitally sampled sound. The sound is so realistic it is difficult to tell it from the sound of actual instruments.

One of the simplest pieces of software available for this new music system is called Kids Time II. The disk has two different programs. First is ABKey, which identifies the letters of the musical scale. The other, called Kids Notes, is an introductory music program. The GS screen graphically displays a five-line musical staff. Notes, bar lines, and other symbols can be moved across the staff with the Apple mouse. On the screen above the staff is a picture of a piano keyboard covering four octaves. When a musical composition is played back, the notes show on the staff. At the same time each note is highlighted on the keyboard in its exact location. The mouse pointer can even be used to play the keyboard something like a real piano.

A professional computer music system has been developed by Electronic Arts. It is named Deluxe Music Construction Set, or DMCS. This is to be combined with a

Software by Mimetics and Electronic Arts provides computer graphics and functions for sound recording and editing.
Left: Screen display of a tape deck.
Right: Displays of an instrumental wave form and "player piano" keyboard.

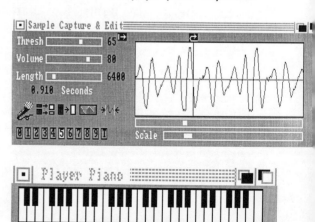

package produced by Mimetics called the Soundscape® Pro MIDI Studio. The combined software forms a complete sound-composing studio that can be used on an Amiga® computer. Most of the software is in the one-hundred-dollar range and the system can be purchased in units and gradually expanded.

DMCS is used for performing and note-writing. Soundscape is used for the recording-studio functions. A MIDI made by Mimetics connects the Amiga digitally with any compatible instrument. And a Sound Digitizer makes it possible to record any sound through a microphone and turn it into an instrumental voice with Soundscape.

The Soundscape system provides some clever graphic features. One is Player Piano, a piano keyboard diagram that shows on screen the notes you have recorded. Another visual is Tape Deck. A picture of a tape recorder appears on the screen with function buttons that can be selected with a cursor just like a real machine. Tape Deck stores the sounds in sequence ready for editing or playback on multiple tracks of sound. Still another computer graphics option is called Wave Form Editor. Suppose you have sampled a clarinet sound with the Digitizer. The exact waveform of the sound shows up on the screen just as it would appear on an electronic oscilloscope screen. By changing the shape of the mathematical peaks and dips of the waveform, the sound itself can be altered.

With the Soundscape system you can also edit the sound *envelope*. This is a contour that looks like a hill or plateau on the screen. Up-slopes represent increases in volume while down-slopes represent decreases. Thus the graphic shape of the envelope determines whether the sound starts with a gentle or sharp attack, whether it falls off quickly in volume, how long the tone sustains, and whether it lasts after a synthesizer key is released. All of this can be edited on the screen even after the sounds are sampled and stored. The Soundscape software with its flexible graphic controls allows sound engineering of recording studio quality.

A new twelve-inch disk recording called *Behind the Mask,* produced by Pree-Mixx Records, is one of the first to be created entirely with the Amiga computer and Soundscape Pro MIDI Studio systems.

□ SCIENCE GRAPHICS □

Even as computer memory storage improves and processing speeds increase, some scientific uses of computers require a volume of stored numbers that becomes almost incomprehensible. At the University of Illinois the National Center for Supercomputing Applications, or NCSA, is helping to solve this problem. The center uses a computer called the Cray X-MP/48. It interfaces with a Macintosh computer. You can set up processing jobs on the Mac. Then no matter where you are, you can send them through NCSA Telenet by computer-linked telephone connection to the Cray. The Cray then processes the material a hundred thousand times faster than could be done with the Mac computer alone.

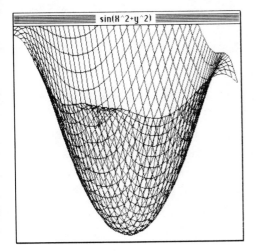
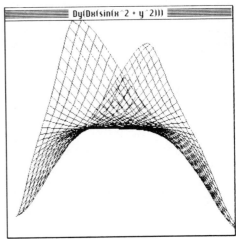

Mathematical figures created with computer graphics using "MacFunction."

Scientists taking advantage of this service will be able to use a new data storage program offered by NCSA. The special program is named Imagetool. It will convert numbers, or bytes, to "images," or megabytes, as the basic unit of stored scientific data. The old saying, "A picture is worth a thousand words," has literally become, "A picture is worth a million words," with the new memory storage program. Imagetool was developed by astrophysicist Mike Norman. He had collected data about streamers of gas in outer space that are called extragalactic jets. Instead of using numbers and graphs or charts, he converted the data to images. For instance, one series of image units showed how the shock wave from an exploding supernova would move through intergalactic clouds to trigger the formation of new stars and galaxies.

Computer graphics has contributed to a new discovery

about the organization of the universe. R. Brent Tully, from the Institute of Astronomy of the University of Hawaii, used a supercomputer to construct maps of how clusters of star galaxies would look to observers at different places in outer space. The computer maps showed that galaxy clusters actually were organized into still larger superclusters. One newly detected supercluster is about one billion light-years long and encompasses about sixty ordinary galaxy clusters, including our own Milky Way.

Computer graphics can help police and investigators to identify faces and find missing people. This is possible because elements of separate photographs can be combined or overlapped on the computer screen. Eyes from one photograph, for example, can be "ghosted" onto the photograph of another face. Or composite elements can be chosen to reconstruct the face of a criminal remembered by a witness. With computerized airbrushing and other techniques, an artist can add a mustache, alter hair and eyebrows, or change facial lines and proportions on any sketch or photograph scanned onto the display screen. In cases of missing children it is possible to artificially age photographs. Thus images released to police and broadcast media more closely resemble the missing youngsters as time passes.

Lillian Schwartz, a specialist at Bell Laboratories in New Jersey, has used such techniques to try to solve a puzzle of the art world. There has always been argument about who was the real model for Leonardo da Vinci's famous painting called the Mona Lisa. There is no record of anyone commissioning the portrait and it is only a guess that it might be of a woman named Mona Lisa Gherardini.

Leonardo loved codes and puzzles. For example, he kept a notebook in which he wrote everything backward so that it would have to be read in a mirror. Ms. Schwartz believes the computer shows that the famous face is none other than that of da Vinci himself. The artist left a known portrait of himself as an old man with a flowing beard. The viewing angle is similar to that of the painting of the Mona Lisa, except that Leonardo is looking slightly to the left instead of to the right.

Using computer graphics, Ms. Schwartz turned over Leonardo's bearded image and juxtaposed it with the face of the Mona Lisa. All of the features matched almost exactly down to the spacing of nose, eyes, and brows. Using the erasing and smoothing feature of her computer graphics system, Ms. Schwartz eliminated the age lines from Leonardo's face. This left a view of Leonardo that was almost a duplicate of the features of the Mona Lisa.

Ms. Schwartz also noticed that embroidery at the neckline of the Mona Lisa was painted to look like the weave of a basket. In Italy baskets were made of a plant called "vinco," a word very similar to Leonardo's last name. Since da Vinci often hid the name of his subject somewhere in each portrait he did, he may have used this stitching to paint his own name into the puzzling portrait of the mysterious woman. In any case the evidence offered through computer graphics lends strong support to the new theory.

Self-portrait by Leonardo da Vinci.   Mona Lisa.

☐   MEDICAL IMAGING   ☐

Computer graphics has also begun to play an important role
in medical imaging. Two types of imaging have already
revolutionized the ability to clearly picture the interior of
the living body. The first is called computerized axial to-
mography, or CAT for short. The part of a patient's body to

Leonardo portrait "flopped" and closely matched
with Mona Lisa by computer graphics.

be photographed is placed within a doughnut-shaped ring.
A series of X-ray images is made from various points around
the doughnut. All X-ray beams pass through the same section of the body but at different angles. A computer analyzes
the combined density readings to produce a cross-sectional
screen image of that part of the body. The image can be
stored and later reproduced photographically.

A second type of scanning system is called nuclear magnetic resonance imaging, or NMR for short. With NMR, protons contained in the atoms of the body are first stimulated to line up magnetically. This causes a release of energy that is like a radio broadcast from the body's own cells. A computer collects this information and creates an image that is a cross section of a selected part of the body.

While CAT and NMR computerized scans are surprisingly clear, the technology of computer graphics has now taken imaging several steps further. A multidimensional technique has been engineered by a surgeon named David White, of Stanford University in California. His system is named CEMAX. The new system stores the computer information taken from any number of scans. The total information is correlated into a full three-dimensional image of bones or other internal body parts.

An example is a series of scans of the skull and jawbone of a policewoman who was shot in the face, with damage to the lower right side of her jawbone. The reconstructed CEMAX images show her facial bones from a number of different angles almost as clearly as if a skeleton had been photographed. With the CEMAX system, viewing angles can be chosen and the image can be lighted from any direction to enhance the shades and shadows.

In the jaw image the section destroyed by the gunshot was clearly visible along with fragments of metal that were imbedded in the bone. This view was compared with that of the uninjured left side of the jaw. The repaired right side would need to look like a mirror image of the left side.

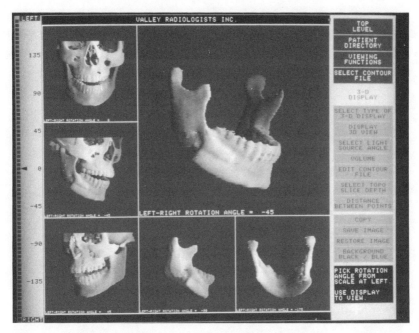

CEMAX multidimensional imaging converts medical scans to a computer image of a jawbone that can be rotated in 3-D.

The last step in the procedure was to use CAM, or computer-aided manufacture, to make a real model of the patient's jaw in exact proportion and detail. Using the solid model, a custom implant was computer-designed. This would fit the policewoman's jaw perfectly when surgery was done later. Such exact computer imaging and CAM modeling has taken much of the guesswork out of reconstructive surgery.

Similar gains in facial plastic surgery have been made using computer graphics. Multiple head photographs can be projected onto a display screen. The views can be altered many times and rotated to suggest the possible appearance following corrective surgery.

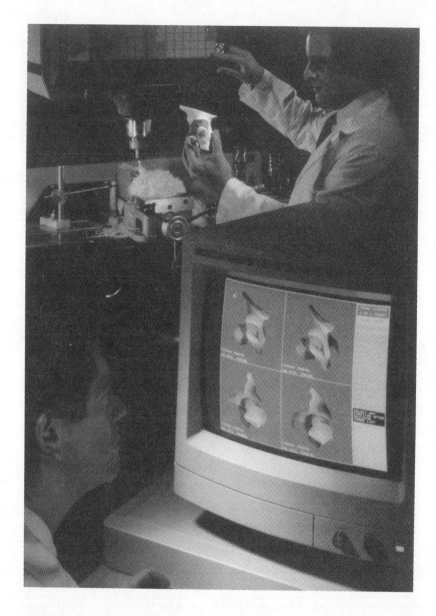

CEMAX 3-D imaging guides automated cutting tools to form an accurate hip bone replacement part for surgical implant.

Another medical use of computer graphics has been for building images of complex biological molecules. Researchers have always used laboratory models, but these are complicated to construct and wires or braces must be used to hold everything together. When modeled on the computer display screen, atomic units can "float" in position in three-dimensional relationships, and the structure can easily be expanded, deformed, or rearranged.

At the University of California in San Francisco, scientist Robert Langridge has used molecular modeling to test alterations in the shapes of particular molecules that might be useful as anti-cancer drugs. When the shapes are correct, molecules will fit together like a key in a lock. On the computer screen the molecular models can be rotated in space so that an exact fit can be achieved. Successful matching suggests which chemicals can bind tightly. Some of these may be "magic bullets" in the fight against cancer.

Even sports medicine has put computer graphics to work. The U.S. Olympic Committee in Colorado uses high-speed cameras to photograph the athletes tumbling, vaulting, or following some other sports routine. The photographic frames are scanned for computer display and converted to stick figures on the screen.

The animated action can be replayed at any speed. Changes in the action can be made to improve the motion of the figures. These changes in posture or balance can then be analyzed by a coach or other specialist to help an athlete overcome bad habits, reduce strain on joints, and improve performance.

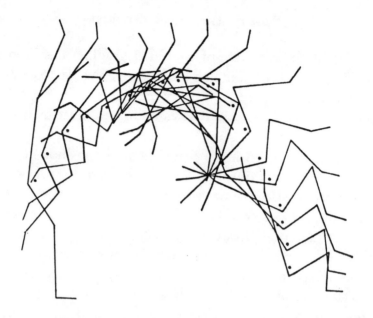

A forward somersault sequence displayed on the computer screen. Animation can be altered to help a gymnast improve his or her performance.

Vision specialists have begun using computer displays for what is called "visual training." Suppose a person has normal vision but a poor ability to react to objects shifting position in space. Or suppose an athlete playing the position of a goalie in hockey wishes to improve his reaction to players on the ice and the fast-moving hockey puck. Whatever the need, an animated visual is designed on the computer graphics screen. In the case of the hockey player, a circle representing the puck moving toward him was displayed repeatedly while he triggered controls to register his mental and physical response. With this visual training the goalie was able to react at the explosive moment when the puck was hit. He felt that this gave him an edge on the ice in actual game conditions.

In such ingenious ways, computer graphics is becoming an important and essential tool in the biological and medical sciences.

4

ANIMATION AND VIDEO GAMES

☐ COLORIZING MOVIES ☐

One of the new uses of computer graphics is adding color to black-and-white movies. One such approach grew out of a plan that was first tried by NASA in 1970. Equipment designers working on the Apollo space mission were forced to save space and weight. Camera designers decided that they could use miniature black-and-white TV cameras instead of color cameras. The images would be colorized later for regular TV broadcast. A cinematographer who had worked on the NASA project later developed the same techniques commercially for a company called Colorization Incorporated.

The colorizing process starts with choosing one film frame from a motion picture that is typical of an extended scene. A mouse or pointer device is used to outline each foreground or background area that is to receive color throughout that scene. Assigned colors are then automatically repeated by computer in the frames that follow, as long as those areas remain part of the scene. When moving objects or figures cross one another in a complicated way, a technician must reassign color areas to avoid confusion. The idea is to program subtle color tones into the flow of images so that the black-and-white contrast remains strong and the effect is of natural color being present.

Colorization can be combined with other computer graphics techniques to alter the appearance of old movies. Contrast can be enhanced. Scratches can be "painted" out. Rough backgrounds can be smoothed, and with good taste color can be blended into the frames so that the result is a movie with the simulated appearance of a color original.

Of course, not all early movies lend themselves to having color added. Colorization is highly controversial, and some movies are best preserved as original black-and-whites. However, colorization means many films will be rediscovered and there will be a wider distribution of films for the home video market that otherwise might not be seen at all.

☐   ANIMATION   ☐

Any sequence of images that suggests motion is said to be animated. Animations range from the very simple to those that are extremely complex; they can be stilted or stylized, or so smooth that figures in motion look completely natural in their movements.

Let us take an example of a very simple animation. Suppose you have a circle drawn with a line on the computer screen. A basic animation would be to move the circle horizontally across the screen. First the circle must be redrawn slightly to the right of its original position. All points representing the circle are moved to the right. The smallest change would be by one pixel on the screen grid. If the circle's coordinate points are continually shifted to the right pixel by pixel, the circle would appear to roll or drift to the right in a series of tiny hops. With a high-resolution screen, the motion would appear almost smooth. The more frequently the circle coordinates are changed, the faster the apparent motion.

Movements upward, at an angle, or in an arc all follow the same principle. Motion is being created in a combination of the two coordinate directions, on the X or horizontal axis and on the Y or vertical axis. When the changes from one position to another, or from one frame to another, are made as rapidly as sixteen per second or faster, the eye and brain no longer perceive them as individual steps, but as blended and continuous motion.

Suppose you now wish the circle to look as if it is moving toward you. Then the circle must be redrawn in a series in which each image is slightly larger than the previous one. The circle appears to grow. Because of three-dimensional perspective, the eye and brain interpret this as motion toward the observer in most cases. By combining computer

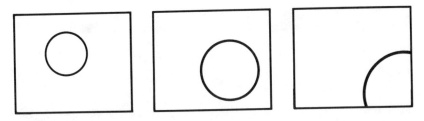

When the circle is shifted and enlarged, it appears to roll past the observer in smooth animation.

commands to shift the circle diagonally sideways with commands to enlarge it, the circle would appear to move both toward you and to the right at the same time. The combined effect is that it has rolled past you on the right.

Each type of change involved in the image is called a parameter. The task of an animation program is to handle all such parameters in an interrelated way.

One of the most advanced computer animation labs in the country is at the New York Institute of Technology on Long Island. There part of the work is pure research. The rest goes into production of commercial projects such as TV ads and feature-length films.

In traditional film animation there are several essential steps. First, general action sequences are sketched on a story board in outline form. Then head animators draw the major position changes of characters in the film. Transparent "cels" are used to build up the entire image. An unchanging background is overlaid with the transparent layers upon which have been drawn all of the action changes step by step. Other animators draw the steps between the major changes or "cycles" drawn by the head animators. Still other artists paint or fill in the characters to look solidly colored.

Shadows, highlights, and other effects must all be added by hand.

In computer animation a certain amount of material is still drawn by hand and then scanned or copied onto the computer screen. Major position changes are drawn as with traditional animation. But many jobs can now be taken over completely by computer. For example, a background artist traditionally creates the background on the screen. Now a photo can be scanned, or the key elements of the background can be set in place with a tablet and stylus. Then, with a menu of computer commands, larger areas and details can be quickly completed. At NYIT, 256 separate colors are instantly available for the screen. Once selected they can be "painted" in with graphics controls that imitate a drawing pen, a paint brush, a watercolor wash, or even the spray and splatter of an airbrush. Areas can be shaded instantly with a sweep of color or gray, changing from dark to light at the same time if desired. Any section of the image can be duplicated or reflected in reverse symmetry.

To create the animation sequences between the main action frames, a new system called TWEEN comes into play. In one project an action sequence of deer jumping and running in a group was developed at NYIT for a Japanese firm. In one main action frame, for example, a deer has all four hooves on the ground. In the next basic frame the deer's front legs are lifted and the head and body are raised at an angle. The computer is fed the two different deer images, each consisting of the same number of enclosed lines. The

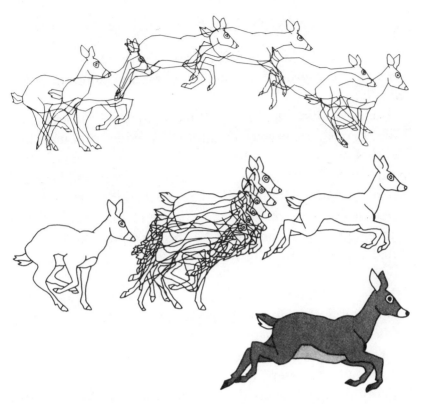

Top and center: "TWEEN" means "in between." The computer automatically fills in a series of animated steps between main positions.
Bottom right: "TWEEP" means "between painting." It is used to fill color areas within the outlines of animated frames.

computer automatically interpolates. That is, it generates a sequence of in-between images that gradually change from the first frame to the next in a smooth series of steps. The TWEEN process is repeated for a series of connections from drawing two to drawing three, and so on through the whole animation. With the jumping deer, the completed sequence was duplicated and the repetitions were overlapped to create the effect of a group of deer bounding and jumping individually.

The next animation step is "ink and paint," nicknamed TWEEP, meaning between painting. Drawings produced by TWEEN are filled in with a selection of fifteen colors, each in fifteen shades (variations of white or black mixed in with the color). Using a table and stylus, the paint artist touches the color selection on a menu with the screen cursor, then touches the area to be filled. All the space within that enclosed outline is rapidly filled with that color and shade choice.

NYIT also boasts an advanced 3-D picture system developed by Sutherland and a colleague named Evans, who worked with him on computer graphics at the University of Utah. With this system data is first stored that represents a top view, front view, and side view of the object, as with CAD. Suppose a spaceship is represented. With the combined data, perspective views can be generated as if one is seeing the spaceship from any desired angle and distance. Then, by the direct action of a joystick, the spaceship image can be made to travel across the screen, turn, move into the distance, turn again, and move back, for example. Or the spaceship can remain stationary while the camera seems to shift or "pan" from right to left or even circle around the ship like a moving observer. At each stage, the computer automatically generates the subtle changes in perspective of the image. Finally, a system similar to TWEEN is used to

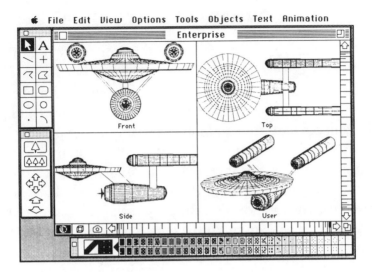

Above: Spacecraft views combined for an animation using Super 3D by Silicon Beach Software.

Below: A Super 3D image rendered completely.

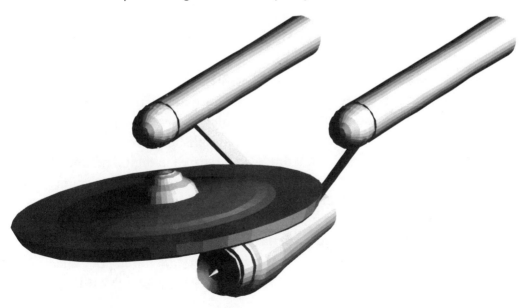

fill in the minute changes between major frames of the action.

Sophisticated animation systems are now employed by commercial advertising agencies and by universities and junior colleges that offer training programs in computer graphics. Such systems include an almost unbelievable number of parameters. For instance, take the animated spaceship example. A basic color for the ship is selected. This can be modified with a choice on the gray scale. One or more light sources can be chosen and assigned position and angle. By dividing the spaceship into many planes or small flat surfaces, the computer determines how the light will reflect from each portion of the curving exterior, whether the surface will appear dull or shiny, where there are highlights from reflected light, and which parts of the spacecraft will be in shadow and to what degree. And as the craft is moved on the display screen, the light and shadow effects will change in a natural way.

All of these effects and controls have become standard on the better equipment. Thus film-making that formerly required solid models and multiple cameras moving along elaborate tracks can now be accomplished directly on the computer screen. The "film" can be stored in digital memory and later reproduced on videotape or motion picture film in smooth and realistic animations of high quality.

A unique problem in computer animation is to record or transfer the individual frames to videotape. For this purpose specialized steps must be followed. First, a "time code" is recorded onto the blank videotape. Next, a signal with no light or color, called a "black burst," is also recorded. The videotape is said to be "stripped." The tape then waits in the videotape recorder, or VCR, in the "park" mode.

Now the animator fills the computer's frame buffer with a single image. The VCR prerolls the tape to a determined location. Then the tape is automatically rewound and started forward again so it is moving at correct speed when it reaches the target location. Through sync timing, the VCR controller activates the record mode so the single frame is recorded onto the videotape at exactly the planned location. The VCR stops. Then it prerolls to the next location, ready to rewind and move ahead for recording the next frame of animation.

In computer animation a full-color image is made of red, green, and blue, or RGB, and is generated digitally. The digital image appears on what is called an RGB monitor and is of high quality, similar to digital sound recorded on a compact disk. In each case the information is free of background signals since any electronic noise in the system is not a part of the information pattern.

American TV sets use what is called an analog color encoding system in accordance with the North American Television Standards Code, or NTSC for short. While this provides an adequate color picture and sound for home use, the analog encoding system is limited in quality in the same way that a long-play record is limited by background noise picked up by the stylus in the turntable arm from material in the record grooves.

To bypass the image noise introduced by NTSC color

encoding, TV commercials or feature presentations are usually made by photographing the digital information from the RGB monitor directly onto 16 or 35 millimeter camera film. This preserves most of the image information and the film itself then serves as a high-quality source.

Lucasfilm Limited, in Marin County, California, is the workshop of moviemaker George Lucas, creator of such films as *Star Wars*. There thirteen computer scientists work with computer graphics effects, some of them the most advanced ever created. New challenges are being tackled all the time.

An example of this creative invention took place with the production of *Star Trek II*. In one part of the movie a wall of fire had to creep around the edge of a planet as it was viewed from space. Programmer Bill Reeves first analyzed the natural components of a burning fire. He decided that all flames shared common characteristics such as color, height, and duration. These characteristics changed through time in a random way. Fire also could be described as a very large number of particles. And these particles could be given varying attributes of color, height, and duration.

For example, the colors red, yellow, and orange were broken down into a broad spectrum of intensities and shades. A wide range of particle trajectories was set up, all of which varied in length and arc. Further, a span of time durations was set up ranging from a fraction of a second to several seconds.

Thus particle *A* might be assigned a color of medium yellow, an angle of five degrees from vertical in a particular curved arc, and a time length of one second. Particle B might be assigned a shade of orange, an angle of seven degrees, a different curve, and a time length of half a second. When enough particles were programmed in this way, they would tend to group and overlap in accidental ways that resembled the flicker of flames licking upward as they appeared and disappeared in a somewhat natural way.

This partly random system is called procedural modeling. It can be applied in many situations where natural variation of elements is needed in a picture. A typical instance is the plants or trees of a forest. All trees have trunks, branches, and leaves, but the sizes, angles, and spacings of these vary from tree to tree. When a wide range of possibilities is stored in memory, a group of trees can be computer-generated on a display screen that resembles the natural differences found in a forest.

This robot ant designed for film by computer animation can be rotated into any position.

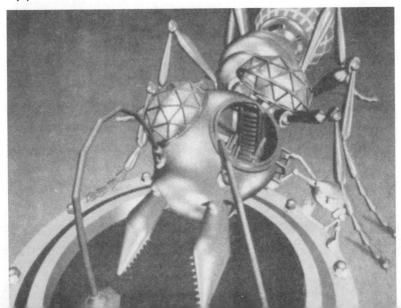

By pushing such animation techniques to their limits, moving images are now being created that are amazingly complete and surprisingly natural. Fantasy films of the future will depend even more on the rapidly changing technology of computer animation.

☐   **COMPUTER SIMULATORS**   ☐

Computer animation is being used to create simulators that train people to operate machines, drive cars, pilot aircraft, and do other complicated jobs. Top Gun is an armed forces training school for pilots of high-performance aircraft, popularized in a movie of the same name. There, computer simulations play a role in helping pilots learn the feel of the aircraft and the reflexes called into play when making decisions at high speed. And of course in modern aircraft computerized displays appear on the instrument panel with changing numbers showing airspeed and altitude and lines showing horizon, attitude or angle, and other information.

One ingenious simulator for training pilots on new aircraft is a helmet with small reflecting screens located at an angle just beyond each eye. Video cameras within the helmet apparatus project on these screens graphics of flying fields, airports as seen from above, and other planes in the air. The student sits in a cockpit that duplicates that of the actual aircraft, holding the joystick and manipulating the controls. As the student turns his or her head to left or right or looks up or down, the giant helmet turns, too. The graphic images projected from inside the helmet shift to match exactly what the trainee would naturally see with the head at that angle.

One of the best-known test pilots in the United States is General Chuck Yeager. Because of his interest in pilot training, Yeager joined forces with a software company named Electronic Arts, makers of both educational and entertainment video games.

With Yeager's advice, a software program was designed by Ned Learner, who wanted to come as close as possible to a $50,000 flight trainer in an inexpensive package for home computer. The collaboration resulted in Chuck Yeager's Advanced Flight Trainer. The software could be used by anyone but was designed especially for those who already knew how to fly an airplane.

The main computer view is through the windshield above a standardized instrument panel. Indicators are complete and include such basics as a heading indicator or compass, an altimeter that measures in feet the height of the plane above sea level, both an airspeed indicator and a vertical speed indicator, a throttle power indicator, and a gyroscopic attitude indicator that shows the bank or pitch of the plane relative to the horizon. There are wing flap indicators and even a slip indicator to help coordinate control of the horizontal elevator and vertical aileron of the tail assembly. There is also a meter that shows the number of G forces affecting the pilot if the plane is in a dive.

With Yeager's computer graphics trainer you can choose to test yourself in any of fourteen different aircraft from the small Cesna 172 Skyhawk to the turbojet XPG-12 Samurai.

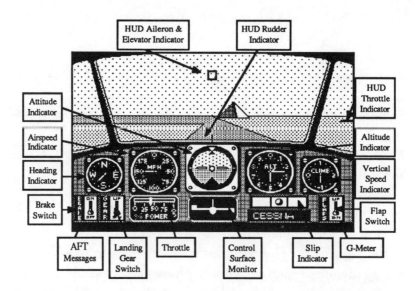

The realistic cockpit display for Chuck Yeager's Advanced Flight Trainer.

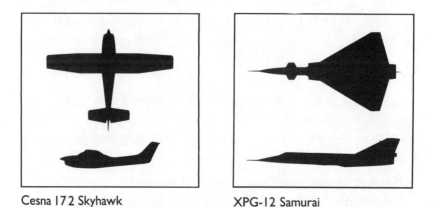

Cesna 172 Skyhawk   XPG-12 Samurai

You have a programmed choice of airports for takeoff and landing, and a set of test pilot procedures. There are high-speed races and special challenges for extra difficulty, such as heavy wind or obstacle courses made up of a series of gates or a corridor between tall buildings. If you want to try aerobatics, you can do formation stunts as you fly side by side with Yeager, whose own control-stick moves are programmed into the software. It is a professional and realistic graphic trainer in which the screen image responds instantly to the moves of your computer unit's joystick. You experience much of the "feel" of actually being in an aircraft.

The popularity of Yeager's computer trainer led Electronic Arts to release a follow-up software package called Chuck Yeager's Advanced Flight Simulator. This graphics package allows the user to experience simulated flight in fourteen more high-performance planes, including the Bell-X-1, the plane in which Chuck Yeager broke the sound barrier.

At NASA's Jet Propulsion Laboratory, Jim Blynn uses computer graphics to simulate the look of outer space. The images are a combination of stored computer data and artist's renderings. When new data is gathered during a flyby mission, such as the one by one of Saturn's moons, the information is used to revise the artist's conceptions. Using the data, complete animated space movies are created with about forty to fifty key frames forming the basis of a five-minute movie. The computer can exaggerate color for clarity or impact, and it can create a motion blur that makes the space image look more realistic.

The NASA computer graphics techniques help to illustrate and compare the goals of competing imaging teams. Decisions and compromises in mission plans can be made. Long before any mission takes place, the computer-generated pictures show what kind of space view can most likely be expected. Selections can be made about which upcoming views deserve camera priority.

☐ **VIDEO GAMES** ☐

One of the most popular uses of computer graphics is for video games. These can be found in the entertainment centers of beach resorts and shopping malls. And as technology improves, games of similar quality are increasingly on the market for home enjoyment. Some games can be used with a standard computer keyboard. Others require a control device such as a mouse. A standard video-game controller is the joystick. This is much like the control device found in an airplane. It can be moved to right or left and away from the player or toward the player in any combination of angles. Movements of a joystick control action on the display screen or control the attitude of a moving vehicle relative to surroundings pictured on the screen.

One new video game is called Beyond Dark Castle, a sequel to the popular Dark Castle. The game is produced for both arcade and home use. The new version has a fast-paced style and animations without flicker. The software is made for Macintosh computers and includes realistic digital sound effects.

To play the game the player uses the keyboard along with the Mac mouse to guide the screen image of the game's

SCORE	117,000	LIVES	2	⊂⊃ KEYS	3
ROCKS	48	BOMBS	5	⋄ ELIXIRS	9
HEALTH	✸✸✸✸✸✸✸✸✸✸■			½ GAS	3

𝔄𝔫𝔱𝔢 𝔕𝔬𝔬𝔪

Beyond Dark Castle

hero, Prince Duncan. Duncan explores the Dark Castle looking for five "Magic Orbs." When Duncan has collected all the Orbs, the player can enter the chambers of the Black Knight for a final battle.

The new Beyond Dark Castle software has the ability to save games that are in progress. Another improvement is full-screen scrolling. As the player guides Duncan across the screen toward the edge of the scene, the entire screen scrolls to show the area Duncan is moving into.

Another video game is Air Traffic Controller. The object is to control air traffic around a particular airport as if the game player is a professional in the control tower. On screen appears a large circle representing the radar display. Airplane symbols enter the radar area on individual flight paths.

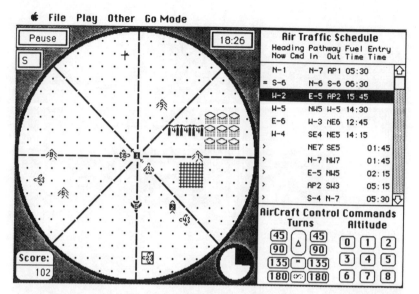

Air Traffic Controller shows the radar display, plane flight paths and altitudes, weather patterns, and flight obstacles. A player must plan landings and takeoffs to avoid collisions.

The player's job is to guide takeoffs and landings, prevent midair collisions, aid the planes in avoiding bad weather, keep them out of restricted zones, and give instructions for avoiding obstacles such as power lines and towers or hills. Each plane must leave the radar sector on the correct course and altitude.

Symbols for weather clouds, power towers, and the moving planes themselves show within the radar circle on the screen. To the right is a table giving compass headings, entry times, and fuel allocated to each aircraft. At the lower right are command numbers for altitude levels 1 through 8, and aircraft turns of 45 degrees, 90 degrees (a right angle), 135 degrees, and a complete 180-degree reverse.

110

The player can choose from up to five airports, and specifies the number of planes involved in the game, their spacing distances, the number of obstacles, the size of restricted zones, and weather that is good, bad, or deadly. Play is condensed into short periods during which he or she makes all decisions about direction and altitude for the various aircraft. Using a mouse, the player first clicks on an airplane, and then clicks on altitude and compass direction settings for that plane. Meanwhile, other planes move in their own directions and weather changes drift unexpectedly into the radar area as the player tries to avoid confusion.

Versions of many sports games have also been adapted to the video screen. Naturally, playing a game on a screen is not the same as being a real athlete on the field, but many of the same situations, plans, dangers, and thrills can be programmed into a well-designed video game. Games in which players or balls move across a field or game surface are good video candidates. The outlines of the field can appear on the screen complete with boxes, circles, and boundaries. If the game is basketball the three-second corridor, the free throw circle, and the three-point circle all figure into the top view of the court. In tennis one sees the doubles court, singles court, service and foul lines, and the net.

Typically, the video-game user controls one or more action players on a team with his joystick unit. This will contain control buttons so that a football quarterback can release a pass or a tennis player can swing at the ball. The computer can play the part of the other player or team if

Superstar Soccer

there is only one user. Balls are caught, thrown, or bounced in various directions in unexpected ways, and the player must react quickly with the joystick and controls to meet the ongoing challenge. Points are won or lost and the score is tallied by computer as the game progresses.

A representative computer field game is Superstar Soccer, developed by Mindscape for the Commodore® and IBM computers. The field is seen on screen in slight perspective. As play moves toward one goal, that half of the playing field fills the entire screen just as if the game player were watching a real game from high in the grandstand. The mesh goal net and field lines show white on the screen against a green background. Players are animated in a stylistic way as they move across the field. The game user acts the part of the coach and the general manager as well as the team players. He or she can "take the field" as a single player to run, shoot, pass, and defend. As a coach the player can plan strategies, select the game lineup, and make substitutions during game play. There is even provision for recruiting and trading players to improve the team's performance.

Some games are a mixture of existing ones with a new twist. An example is Q-Ball. It is similar to pool or billiards—but the game is designed to be played inside a cube. Shots can be made off any wall in all three dimensions. There are eight pockets and the balls bounce inside the cube as if there were no gravity. In addition, the perspective angle of the "table" can be rotated through 262 different viewing angles in 3-D as the player takes a turn. The game is planned for either one or two players. The level of difficulty can be controlled by adjusting spin, friction, and the velocity or power of the shots. Q-Ball is available for both Atari® and Amiga computers.

Programmed instruction is built into a variety of video games for learning experiences both in school and at home. At preschool and elementary levels games like Word Bank, Word Magic, and Wordmaze teach the skills of reading and word recognition. In Word Bank, for instance, the student classifies words according to long and short vowels or everyday experiences as he or she visits a toy store, a pet shop, or a grocery store. Screen visuals set the scene and words are inserted by the player. In Word Magic up to six students learn consonants and how to build large words from shorter words by playing a game of traveling through Camelot. Each player can only continue travel by creating new words from his or her root words. Skills in mathematics are covered in special ways, from the addition, subtraction, multiplication, and division required in a game like Space Math to a more difficult series for middle grades called Success With Algebra.

Video packages can be purchased for learning other skills. Behind the Wheel teaches young students how to follow simple map directions. At a higher level, both youngsters and adults can use a package called Keys to Responsible Driving to learn traffic safety, driving regulations, and road signs, as well as practical skills in handling and maneuvering a vehicle through town and city streets.

Keys to Responsible Driving

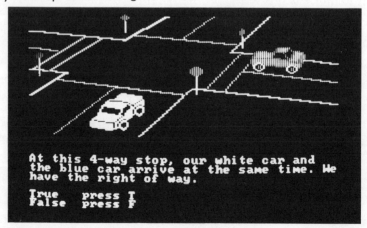

114

The Sea Voyagers

Map skills lend themselves naturally to the graphics screen. Students can draw political boundaries, name geographic regions, and recognize island and continental land masses. Frequently mapping is combined with history. A good example is a game called The Sea Voyagers, marketed for Apple and IBM computers. In the game are four activities to help students understand the expeditions of famous explorers like Columbus, Magellan, Verrazzano, and Cortez, along with the social and cultural changes that followed their discoveries.

In entertaining and educational games like these, video-game designers combine the advantages of computer graphics, computer animation, programmed instruction, and user control to achieve an ongoing variety of software that can be both fun and practical.

AFTERWORD:
GRAPHICS FOR THE FUTURE

An important trend in computer graphics is miniaturization. This technology comes not only from pure research but from interrelated fields like space exploration, image processing, CAD design, cartography, desktop publishing, and other disciplines. Actually, all branches of science using electronics eventually share any developments that make more functions available in less space with fewer components and controls. Thus future computer memories will occupy less space, image-generating units will be more compact with flatter screens, and most computer graphics equipment will be more portable. Already one of these trends is evident in the flat display screen developed by Zenith, called Zenith Perfect Monitor.

The natural offshoot of improved electronics is mass production of computer components with more sophisticated and more flexible capabilities. Therefore, the general trend is toward better quality at lower prices. Computers will be more "intelligent." More commands will be automated. And the functions once found only in larger professional systems will all be available to the amateur. This means that more young people both at home and in schools and other facilities will have a chance to use excellent computer graphics equipment. Computer graphics skills will become commonplace. The computer screen is becoming literally the sketchbook, drawing board, artist's easel, and design shop of the future.

As better technology becomes affordable, improved screen images will become the norm. For example, the NeXT computer developed by Steve Jobs, co-founder of Apple Computer, already offers the college teacher or serious home user a very high resolution nineteen-inch CAD display, along with internal memory and erasable disk storage that exceeds most long-term educational requirements. At the same time printers of all sorts, from dot-matrix to thermographic and laser printers, will yield much higher resolution. Indeed, new types of printers creating images with fewer steps and less complicated mechanics will certainly be invented. Even in low-cost units, pictures will no longer have any sort of "computer" look but will be of the same quality as professional photography.

Still another trend is toward more compatability. The size of floppy disks is rapidly being standardized from the old 5.25-inch size to the smaller 3.5-inch size. New IBM computers now use a mouse similar to the one made for

Macintosh computers. At the same time the newer Macintosh SE and Macintosh II computers can use any software that is on 3.5-inch disks. It is expected that shortly there will be products to easily interconnect unrelated systems such as IBM and Macintosh. So differences between computers and computer graphics systems made by various manufacturers are becoming less important. This means that whatever equipment is used to learn computer graphics, the skills will be easily transferable to almost any other equipment, without relearning commands and procedures.

Animation for TV and film is becoming faster and less costly with computer graphics. In the future even full-length films will rely almost entirely on computer-generated programs, digitized 3-D models, and computer action sequences.

Today laser holography is being researched and improved. Holograms are 3-D images that can be examined from all sides like real objects as observers shift their viewing locations. Holographic theater projection is on the verge of practical solution. Indeed, holographic imaging is already being tested as an extension of computer graphics in medical scanning. Improvements in holographic technology will not only make totally three-dimensional moving picture films a reality, but totally realistic computer images as well. Just as in current science fiction, films won't be confined to a projection screen; eventually a solid-looking moving image will be generated in the middle of a room. The observer will be able to walk around and observe the action from any chosen angle. Such images will be stored, altered, and communicated from location to location with unbelievable speed, flexibility, and accuracy.

As unlikely as it seems, most of these trends in computer graphics are predictable from science that already exists. Future discoveries will speed this process in ways difficult to imagine but as certain as the progress of human invention. Such is the exciting future we can expect in the fascinating world of computer graphics.

GLOSSARY

BASIC: Acronym for *B*eginner's *A*ll-purpose *S*ymbolic *In*struction *C*ode; a popular high-level computer language
Binary: Using only the digits 0 and 1 to express all numbers
Bit: Short for "binary digit"; has a value of either 0 or 1
Bit map: Image converted to a grid matrix represented by binary digits stored in computer memory
Buffer memory: A computer's temporary memory-storage component
Byte: Binary unit usually made up of eight bits
CAD: Computer-aided design
CAM: Computer-aided manufacture
Cathode-ray tube (CRT): Vacuum tube with a viewing screen; generates an electron beam from a heated cathode
Compiler: Computer program translating a high-level language into machine language

Controller: Device that calculates, places, and moves elements on the computer screen

Coordinates: Numerical positions on a grid represented along horizontal and vertical lines

Cursor: Movable control marker on a display screen; target device for tracing and digitizing

Data: Information processed or generated by computer

Digitizing: Using only the numerical values 0 and 1 to represent a graphic image in computer code

Disk: Flat, rotating magnetically coated plate used for storing information

FORTRAN: Acronym for *for*mula *tran*slation; a high-level computer language designed for scientific and engineering computations

Graphics: Images used for communications by means of computer display, print, or film

Grid: Pattern of rectangles formed by intersecting horizontal and vertical lines; useful for text graphics, image graphics, and coordinate locations

Hard copy: Image output of a computer system, generated by plotter, printer, or camera film

Hardware: The physical components of a computer system

Joystick: Vertical lever whose multiple motions control the disposition of elements on a computer screen

Kilobyte (K): 1,024 bytes, or approximately 1,000 bytes of computer memory

Language: Code system by which people communicate with computers

Light Pen: Light-sensitive tool used to move a cursor or enter commands when held near a computer screen

Machine code: Elementary level of binary code used for computer function

Megabyte (M): $1,024^2$, or approximately one million bytes of computer memory

Monitor: CRT or storage tube device used for graphic display

Mouse: Rolling-ball device translating hand motion to movements of cursor on display screen

Pascal: High-level computer language named for Blaise Pascal

Pixel: Short for "picture element"; smallest displayable spot on a computer screen

QWERTY: Standard typewriter-style keyboard, named for the first six letters in the third row of keys

Raster: Modality that "rakes" or scans an image

Software: Any program designed to control computer tasks; usually available on floppy or hard disk

Tablet: Work surface transmitting stylus motion to display screen

Terminal: Combined input-output device, such as a computer display screen and keyboard

VCR: Video cassette recorder

Wireframe: 3-D object that is represented in terms of its edges

Workstation: Group of interrelated computer components, consisting of a display screen and keyboard, disk drive, control devices, linkage to image input and output, and usually linkage to a host computer

WORM: "*Write Once Read Many*"; laser disk for storing computer data

Zoom: To enlarge or magnify a section of computer image, as with a zoom lens

INDEX

Illustrations appear in **boldface.**